SAYING & SEEING

SAYING & SEEING

*20 Nuggets About Speaking
God's Word*

ROZELIA HARRIS

XULON PRESS

Xulon Press
2301 Lucien Way #415
Maitland, FL 32751
407.339.4217
www.xulonpress.com

Scripture quotations taken from the Amplified® Bible (AMP). Copyright © 2015 by The Lockman Foundation. Used by permission. All rights reserved.

Scripture quotations taken from the Amplified® Bible (AMPC), Copyright © 1954, 1958, 1962, 1964, 1965, 1987 by The Lockman Foundation. Used by permission.

Scripture quotations taken from the King James Version (KJV) – *public domain*.

Scripture quotations taken from the New American Standard Bible (NASB). Copyright © 1960, 1962, 1963, 1968, 1971, 1972, 1973, 1975, 1977, 1995 by The Lockman Foundation. Used by permission. All rights reserved.

Scriptures marked YLT are Scripture quotations from the Young's Literal Translation of the Bible (Public Domain).

Printed in the United States of America.

Paperback ISBN-13: 978-1-66280-004-7
eBook ISBN-13: 978-1-6628-0005-4

TABLE OF CONTENTS

SECTION TWO: SPEAKING TRUTHS ABOUT YOUR WORDS 41

PREFACE

This book is prefaced with the following:

1. This book is about the words that we speak, which we believe (are convinced of). The words that come out of the abundance of our heart.

2. The term "Word of God" means God's Word from the Bible.

3. The "Word of the Lord" is the same as the Word of God. Jesus stated in John 12:49 that He only spoke what the Father said. What Jesus spoke was the Word of God.

4. The term "WORD" is referring to the Word of God.

5. Section Three of the book is about Job, and it is not to find fault with Job. The Book of Job is like all other books in the Bible. It is given to provide doctrine, reproof, correction, and instruction. There is a lot we can learn about our words from the Book of Job.

6. A scripture, or portion of scripture, can demonstrate several spiritual truths. Some of the biblical accounts in this book that will demonstrate more than one Speaking Truth include the 10 spies and the promised land, the birth of *John the Baptist*, the centurion's servant, Abraham and Sarah, David and Goliath, and the woman with the issue of blood.

Introduction

THIS BOOK HAS 20 NUGGETS ABOUT SPEAKING, and the importance of speaking the Word of God, and speaking in agreement with the Word of God so that we experience what God desires for our lives and His kingdom. According to Colossians 1:13, God has delivered Christians from the power of darkness and translated us into the kingdom of His dear Son (Jesus). When we are born again, we have newness of life in this kingdom. We have to learn to live and function in this kingdom, and that includes learning to speak the language of this new kingdom. The Kingdom of God has a language and it is the Word of God.

Growing up, I heard songs in church about things being new when one is born again (a new way of talking was in some of those songs). This is true, we should be speaking a certain way. Psalm 107:2 says, "Let the redeemed of the LORD say so, whom he hath redeemed from the hand of the enemy."[1] The one the Lord has redeemed should be saying something. The Christian should be speaking in agreement with the things of their redemption, but this new way of speaking is not automatic. We have to purpose to do this. The Lord approached Abraham and told him how to speak in Genesis 17:5. Abraham's name was still Abram at the time, and the

Lord told him to start calling himself Abraham, which meant the father of a multitude. Abraham had to learn to speak a certain way to experience the promise of God. The Lord has done the same thing for us that he did for Abraham. He has given us information about words and instruction about how we should be speaking in His Word.

There are many scriptures in the Book of Proverbs alone that provide revelation and instruction about our speaking and words. Some of the scriptures in Proverbs, Psalms, and Ecclesiastes that provide insight about our words include those referencing man's lips, tongue, mouth, words, saying, and speaking.

Let's read a few such scriptures from Psalm and Proverbs:

> [14]A man will be satisfied with good by the fruit of his words, And the deeds of a man's hands will return to him.
> Proverb 12:14, NASB

> [23]Whoso keepeth his mouth and his tongue keepeth his soul from troubles.
> Proverbs 21:23, KJV

> [6]The words of the wicked lie in wait for blood, But the mouth of the upright will deliver them.
> Proverbs 12:6, NASB

> [19]When there are many words, transgression is unavoidable, But he who restrains his

lips is wise.
Proverbs 10:19, NASB

[12]Who is the man who desires life And loves
length of days that he may see good?
[13]Keep your tongue from evil And your lips
from speaking deceit.
Psalm 34:12-13, NASB

[18]There is one who speaks rashly like the
thrusts of a sword, But the tongue of the wise
brings healing.
Proverbs 12:18, NASB

[21]Death and life are in the
power of the tongue,
And those who love it will eat its fruit.
Proverbs 18:21, NASB

Notice in these scriptures that satisfaction in life, seeing good in life, preventing trouble in life, having many good days, and even deliverance from trouble was connected to words. According to Proverbs 18:21, death and life are in the power of the tongue (your speaking, your words, what you say). This scripture along is evidence that your words have tremendous power.

The word for "word" is sometimes translated "thing."[2] Words are considered things. Words are things, and they produce what they are. If your words are words of sickness, then they produce sickness. If your words are words of health, then they produce health. If your words are words of poverty, then you will be impoverished or have lack. Think about how the words in a sad song have the ability to cause someone to experience the emotion of sadness. It's the result of words.

Chapter 3 in the Book of James expounds on how a man's tongue works in his life, similar to the way a bit does in a horse's mouth and a rudder does on a ship. The bit controls the direction the horse goes, while the rudder controls the direction of the ship. Likewise, a person's tongue can control the direction or path of that person's life. You can deliberately use your tongue to direct the path of your life and you can use it to direct your life towards seeing many good days.

Some may think that James 3:7-8 denotes that we can't control our speaking, or tame the tongue.

> [7]For every kind of beasts, and of birds, and
> of serpents, and of things in the sea, is tamed,
> and hath been tamed of mankind:
> [8]But the tongue can no man tame; it is an
> unruly evil, full of deadly poison.
> James 3:7-8, KJV

James 3:7-8 speaks of how mankind has managed to tame birds, beast, reptiles, and other creatures but can't tame the tongue. A key word here is "tamed." When these beasts, fowl, reptiles, and creatures are tamed, their state of existence is changed. When these creatures are tamed, the one who tamed the creature has accomplished the goal and finished the job. The job of taming is complete. In most cases, these creatures cannot survive if placed in their natural habitat, after they have been tamed. James is not saying that man can't do anything about the tongue. There are too many scriptures that set forth what we should and should not say. Therefore, James 3:7-8 can't mean that man is not able to do anything about the tongue. Man can't tame the tongue the way mankind can tame beasts, fowl, reptiles, and creatures of the sea. You can't do something to the tongue and "voila" you're done, your tongue is now altered (tamed) and set for life. The tongue does not get tamed like this. You always have to guard it. There is a requirement for our entire lives to deliberately guard the words that come out of our mouths. When we speak, we are to speak with a deliberate, desired, intentional outcome in mind that agrees with the Word of God.

Additional confirmation that James 3:7-8 cannot mean one can't do anything about the tongue is in James 3:9-10.

⁸But the tongue can no man tame; it is an
unruly evil, full of deadly poison.
⁹Therewith bless we God, even the Father;
and therewith curse we men, which are made
after the similitude of God.
¹⁰Out of the same mouth proceedeth blessing
and cursing. My brethren, these things ought
not so to be.
James 3:8-10, KJV

Here, James himself is saying you should not use the tongue to bless and curse. This means the person has the ability to not speak both blessing and cursing out of the same mouth. Man may not be able to tame the tongue, but we can control the tongue. Another example, from James himself, about the ability to control our tongue is in James 1:26, where he communicates that the religion of the one who does not bridle his tongue is worthless. There is an assumption here that the person can bridle their tongue. These are confirmations that James could not have meant in absolute terms that man can't control his tongue.

Your words are the things that you have in your life. I'll phrase it this way, there are things that you have in your life right now that are words (things) you have believed in your heart and have spoken. If you are not accustomed to believing that your words are things and that they have power, you will have to renew your mind to this truth. Imagine if we all operated in this truth as the Body of Christ (if we would intentionally function knowing that our words have power, and begin to believe and speak in accordance with God's plans and purposes for the Church of the Lord Jesus Christ).

Since Psalm 34:12-13 is the foundational scripture for the book, let's spend some time on it.

> ¹²Who is the man who desires life And loves
> *length of* days that
> he may see good?
> ¹³Keep your tongue from evil And your lips
> from speaking deceit.
> Psalm 34:12-13, NASB

Psalm 34:12-13 imparts for us that the person who wants to be pleased with life and see many good days has to do something. Verse 13 points out that the person has to refrain from saying certain things. The first thing that person has to refrain from speaking is evil (disaster, adversity, harm, affliction, hurt, ruin, trouble, unpleasant things, distress, misery, sorrow, calamity, displeasure, and injury).[3] The second thing that person has to refrain from speaking is deceit (treacherously or falsely).[4] Treachery is a violation of faith.[5] The person who wants to be pleased with life and see many good days is one who keeps their lips from speaking things that are false (not the truth) or things that are treacherous (not of faith). Jesus said that God's Word is Truth.[6] If you don't want to speak falsely, then speak the Word of God, so that you are speaking truth. This person will also not speak in violation of faith. Since God's Word produces faith, His Word has to be words of faith. Romans 10:8 speaks of the word of faith. Speaking the Word of God is speaking words of faith. From Psalms 34:12-13 we can decipher that the person who is going to be pleased with life and see many good days is the one who speaks a certain way. Hence, the title of the book, "*Saying and Seeing.*" Your speaking is connected to what you see (have and experience) in your life.

When we look at the importance of our words from a spiritual point, far too often there is resistance. The world knows words have power and functions in the power of words every day. If words do not have power, why are there motivational speakers whose purpose is to use their words (speaking) to motivate people to act a certain way or do a certain thing? Why are there political speeches made for the purpose of motivating people to support a specific candidate? Why are there ads or commercials on radio (things that are audible) for the purpose of persuading the listener to purchase something or support something? The answer is obvious, words have power and speaking is occurring in all these instances to yield or produce a certain outcome or results.

The purpose of this book is to share information from the Word of God that demonstrates how our words can contribute to what we see (have and experience) in our lives. For those of you now thinking, "*I thought faith causes what we see in our lives,*" you are correct, but speaking is a component of faith. The 20 nuggets in the book have been titled Speaking Truths. One of those will cover the relationship between faith and speaking. The book has three Sections; Speaking Truths about God's Word, Speaking Truths about Your Words, and a Speaking Truth from the Book of Job. These Speaking Truths will help you learn the importance of words and the benefit of speaking God's Word.

SPEAKING TRUTHS ABOUT GOD'S WORD

GOD SHARES WITH US IN DEUTERONOMY 8:3 THAT man is to live by His Word and in Joshua 1:8 that we are to keep the Word of God on our lips. Since we are to live by God's Word, and since speaking God's Word is a component of good success, we should become acquainted with some truths about His Word. This section will provide truths that will build your faith in God's Word and help you understand the benefits of keeping God's Word on your lips. This section has 8 Speaking Truths.

GOD'S WORD IS A CREATIVE FORCE

SCRIPTURE DOCUMENTS IN GENESIS 1:1 THAT God had created the heavens and the earth. Then, in Genesis 1:2 the earth is now without form and empty. Jeremiah 4:23-26 portrays for us that something happened to the earth to cause this condition that we see in Genesis 1:2. Jeremiah depicts how the earth had mountains, hills, and had been a fruitful land. Then he sees it as a wilderness. When you read Jeremiah 4:23-26, note that verse 25 mentions there was no man. The earth, at some point before there was man had mountains, hills and was a fruitful land. There was a time before Genesis 1:2 when the earth was not without form and empty.

In Genesis 1:2, God is seeing something that He does not want. He's seeing this earth without form and empty. He's seeing water covering the earth and He's seeing darkness. But things begin to change in Genesis 1:3-4. God begins to see something different. What happened to cause this change? God begins to do something to cause what He was seeing to change. Studying what God does in Genesis to change what

He was seeing from what He did not want to see to what He desired to see will illustrate God's method of doing things.

In Genesis 1:3, God said, "Let light be" and in Genesis 1:4 God saw light.[7] There was darkness, however God wanted light interjected into this situation. He wanted something different from what He was seeing, so what did God do to change things? He spoke what He wanted. Since He wanted light manifesting, He spoke about light. In Genesis 1:9 God wanted to see something different with the water. He spoke for the waters to be gathered in one place, and for the dry land to be seen. Once God saw this, He called the waters seas and the land earth. God wanted something done concerning the waters and He spoke something to make it happen.

God wants to begin seeing grass, herbs, and fruit trees. What did He do to start seeing this? Read Genesis 1:11 below for the answer.

> [11]And God said, Let the earth bring forth
> grass, the herb yielding seed, and the fruit
> tree yielding fruit after his kind, whose seed
> is in itself, upon the earth: and it was so.
> Genesis 1:11, KJV

God spoke something when He wanted to see grass, herbs and fruit trees and Genesis 1:12 reports that He saw it. Even when it came to creating man. God desired a man for this earth, and He did not see one. To change this, He said in Genesis 1:26 "Let us make man in our image, after our likeness:"[8] He spoke about man to start seeing a man. Are you beginning to see the pattern? God's method of changing what He does not want to see to what He does want to see (or have), is speaking.

There is something else to be grasped while reviewing these creation scriptures. God was not continually speaking how things were or what He did not want to see. He did not keep saying over and over, "*It's dark.*" He did not say over and over, "*There are no animals.*" He did not say over and over, "*I'm tired of seeing water and why is this water every-where?*" People can sound similar to this when they continually speak about the thing they don't want to see, as opposed to speaking what they want to see. Instead of speaking over and over how things were and what He did not want to see, God spoke what He wanted to see, and God saw what He spoke. God's method of causing things to change to what He wanted to see was speaking. The way God does things is through speaking. God does things through words and He has given mankind the same ability.

The Word of God not only demonstrates how this method of "saying and seeing" happens for God, it also documents how it happens for people. It happened for a man named David. In I Samuel 17:46, David said the following to Goliath.

> [46]This day will the LORD deliver thee into mine hand; and I will smite thee, and take thine head from thee; and I will give the car-cases of the host of the Philistines this day unto the fowls of the air, and to the wild beasts of the earth; that all the earth may know that there is a God in Israel.
> I Samuel 17:46, KJV

David was speaking this way based on believing the Word of God about Israel being the descendants of Abraham and having a covenant with the living God. As Abraham's descendants they were supposed to defeat their enemies.[9] I Samuel 17:50-53 confirms that David saw what he said. David killed Goliath and cut off his head, and the army of Israel defeated the Philistines. David said and he saw.

Mark 5:25-34 records one of the accounts of Jesus healing a woman who had a blood condition for 12 years. She went to many physicians and spent all her money, but only got worse. She heard of Jesus and began saying, "If I only touch His garment, I will get well."[10] The Amplified Bible Classic Edition states that she kept saying the statement. The woman spoke about getting well and she saw healing in her life. She said and she saw.

It happened for a virgin named Mary, in Luke Chapters 1 and 2. The angel Gabriel spoke to Mary, saying that she would conceive and bring forth the Messiah (Jesus). In response to Gabriel, Mary said the following, "Be it unto me according to thy word."[11] Mary is with child in Luke Chapter 2:4-5, and in Luke 2:7 she brings forth Jesus. Mary spoke for it to be done to her according to the Word, and that is what she saw. She agreed with the Word of God happening to her. She did not speak against or opposite the Word of God. What you believe and say is also what is done to you. If you want it to be the Word of God, then you can't believe and speak against the Word of God.

You can most likely look back over your life and see instances of what you said coming to pass. You said something and you saw it happen in your life. I can definitely do that with my life. I thought about the number of times that I watched award shows, or interviews of celebrities or athletes, and how often one of them would say, "*I always said I would be famous,*" or "*I always said I would make it,*" or "*I always said I could do this.*" I've even heard some say they kept saying they could do something when others told them they could not, and even when it appeared they could not.

God's Word is not only a creative force for Him, God's Word in your heart and in your mouth can create God's desired outcomes in your life and for the Church of the Lord Jesus Christ.

GOD'S WORD DOES NOT RETURN VOID

IN ISAIAH 55:10-11 GOD USES THE RAIN AND SNOW to describe an aspect of His Word.

> ¹⁰For as the rain and snow come down from the heavens, and return not there again, but water the earth and make it bring forth and sprout, that it may give seed to the sower and bread to the eater,
> ¹¹So shall My word be that goes forth out of My mouth: it shall not return to Me void [without producing any effect, useless], but it shall accomplish that which I please *and* purpose, and it shall prosper in the thing for which I sent it.
> Isaiah 55:10-11, AMPC

The rain and snow does not fall from the sky and begin a trek upward again. Instead, they continue downward until they water the earth. Watering the earth is not all that happens. Once the rain and snow waters the earth, the earth then brings forth sprouts and gives seed. And that is not all, the seed is provided for the sower and bread is provided for eating. All of this happens as a result of the rain and snow coming down. The rain and the snow comes down for a purpose, to produce certain things or make certain things happen. The Lord said His Word works the same way. His Word does not go out of His mouth and return without producing something. Verse 11 conveys what God's Word produces. His Word produces exactly what God spoke. God's Word accomplishes the purpose for which He speaks it.

Luke Chapter 5 starts with the Lord Jesus using the boat of a fisherman named Peter, to teach people the Word of God. Afterwards, Jesus directs Peter to move the boat to deeper water and put out his fishing nets for a catch. Peter recounts how he and others had worked all night and caught nothing. Despite this, Peter says to the Lord, "Nevertheless at thy word I will let down the net."[12] Peter puts a net into the water and he began catching so many fish that he had to call for another boat to help. The Lord's Word (which is the same as God's Word) about catching fish did not return void, but accomplished the purpose for which it was spoken.

The Lord told Peter to put nets (plural) in the water, but Peter only put one net in the water. The Lord spoke for Peter to lower nets, because He knew His Word was not returning void and that nets would be needed for this catch. I see seed time and harvest in this account. Peter sowed his boat for Jesus to fish for men and Peter got a harvest of fish (an instant miraculous harvest of fish). This was one of those Amos 9:13

harvest. Peter's seed of sowing use of his boat for the Lord's work yielded a harvest the same day. We talk about receiving a harvest in the same year, this was a harvest in the same day. Glory!!!

The 3rd Chapter of the Book of Exodus documents how the children of Israel (the descendants of Abraham) were slaves in Egypt. The Lord God commanded a man named Moses to go and inform the Pharaoh of Egypt and the children of Israel that He was freeing them from slavery and bringing them into the land that He had promised Abraham to give his descendants. This land was good real estate, but it was inhabited by other people. The children of Israel were to be freed from slavery first and then go live in this land. The Word of God spoken in Exodus 3:10 to free them from slavery and the Word spoken in Exodus 3:17 to give them the promised land were both accomplished. You can read about how the children of Israel were freed from bondage by the mighty hand of the Lord in Exodus Chapters 7 through 12, and about them in the promised land in Joshua Chapter 24. The children of Israel were in bondage for 400 years, and the Word of God to free them and give them their own land did not return void. It accomplished the purpose for which the Lord spoke it. It's exciting to know that the Word of God can actually cause people living in bondage to be made free.

There are many scriptures in the Word of God that foretold things about the coming of Jesus the Messiah. They are referred to as Messianic prophecies and were spoken over thousands of years. These scriptures are good confirmations of this Speaking Truth that God's Word does not return void.

Some of the things spoken by God's prophets about the coming Messiah (Jesus Christ) included:

1) A virgin bringing forth the Messiah
2) His being born in Bethlehem
3) His being betrayed for 30 pieces of silver
4) His suffering the death penalty for the sins of mankind
5) His being raised from the dead
6) His ascension to heaven after being raised from the dead.

The list below provides scriptures where God had these 6 Messianic prophecies spoken and where His Word did not return to Him void..

1. *Prophecy that a virgin would bring forth the Messiah.*

   Prophecy Spoken: Isaiah 7:14.
   Word of God where Prophecy Came to Pass: Luke 1:26-56; Luke 2:1-7.

2. *Prophecy that the Messiah would be born in Bethlehem.*

   Prophecy Spoken: Micah 5:2.
   Word of God where Prophecy came to Pass: Matthew 2:1.

3. *Prophecy that the Messiah would be betrayed for 30 pieces of silver.*

   Prophecy Spoken: Zechariah 11:12-13.

Word of God where Prophecy came to Pass: Matthew 26:14-16.

4. *Prophecy that The Messiah would suffer the death penalty.*

Prophecy Spoken: Isaiah 53:7-8.
Word of God where Prophecy came to Pass: Luke 23:39-47.

5. *Prophecy that the Messiah would be raised from the dead.*

Prophecy Spoken: Psalm 16:9-10.
Word of God where Prophecy came to Pass: Mark 16:1-7.

6. *Prophecy that the Messiah would ascend to heaven.*

Prophecy Spoken: Psalm 68:18-20.
Word of God where Prophecy came to Pass: Luke 24:36-51.

I encourage you to read Messianic scriptures in your Bible that have come to pass to continue to build your faith in this Speaking Truth that God's Word does not return void.

God's Word Produces Faith

ROMANS 10:17 ACQUAINTS US WITH THE SPIRItual truth that God's Word produces faith.

> ¹⁷So then faith cometh by hearing,
> and hearing by the word of God.
> Romans 10:17, KJV

The account of Abraham and his wife Sarah is the first example of this Speaking Truth. The Lord spoke to Abram (Abraham's name before it was changed) about having many descendants and being a great nation. The Lord first mentions this to Abram in Genesis 12:1-3 and He speaks it to him again in Genesis 15:1-5 and Genesis 17:15-19. When Abram is 99 and Sarai (his wife) is 90 and barren, the Lord instructs both to change their names. Abram's new name is Abraham, and it meant "father of a multitude."[13] Sarai's new name is Sarah, and meant "a queen."[14] Genesis 17:15-16 explains that her name was changed to this because kings would come from her. The Word of the Lord gave them faith to change their names, regardless of their age and Sarai being barren. As they spoke the Word of the Lord by calling themselves the *"father of a multitude"* and *"a queen from whom kings would come"* it gave them faith. They went from being very old, barren, and a couple without the promised heir to being a very, very, very old couple with a newborn named Isaac.[15] The Lord's Word gave them faith to begin saying what the Lord said about them and they saw His Word about having an heir come to pass.

In Genesis 6:13-17 God approached a man named Noah about building an ark, as He disclosed to Noah that floodwaters were coming on the earth. This Word God spoke to Noah gave him faith to build the ark. Not only did Noah have faith to build the ark, he also had faith to put creatures on the ark. Hebrews 11:7 further confirms that the Word of God gave Noah faith. This scripture says, "By faith Noah, being warned *by God* about things not yet seen, in reverence prepared an ark for the salvation of his household,…"[16] Noah had faith after being warned of something. Who gave Noah the warning? God did. God spoke this warning to Noah and God's Word gave Noah faith.

The angel Gabriel came to Mary in Luke Chapter 1 and told her that she was going to birth the Messiah. This Word from Gabriel to Mary was the Word of God. What Gabriel was speaking was what the Lord spoke by His prophet in Isa 7:14 about a virgin bearing a son. The angel relays to Mary things about her future. This future included her having a Son, naming Him Jesus, Jesus having the throne of David, and having a Kingdom that would not end. Gabriel also told Mary that her cousin Elizabeth (who was very old and barren) was now with child. This Word of God spoken to Mary by the angel Gabriel produced faith in Mary.

How do we know that Mary had faith in this Word? We know from these things:

1) By what was spoken coming to pass
2) By Mary acting on the Word and going to visit her cousin Elizabeth
3) By what Elizabeth spoke to Mary in Luke 1:45 when she said, "And blessed is she that believed: for there shall be a performance of those things which were told her from the Lord."[17]

This statement by Elizabeth confirms that Mary had faith in what was told her from the Lord.

God's Word is a Seed and How the Kingdom of God Functions

JESUS PREACHED AND TAUGHT THE KINGDOM OF God. He used parables to teach some aspects of the Kingdom. Two of the parables that reveal some truths about the Kingdom of God are the *"Parable of the Sower"* and the *"Parable of the Growing Seed."* Both explain things about the role that the Word of God has in the Kingdom of God. Read about the *"Parable of the Sower"* below.

> [5]A sower went out to sow his seed: and as he sowed, some fell by the way side; and it was trodden down, and the fowls of the air devoured it.
> [6]And some fell upon a rock; and as soon as it was sprung up, it withered away, because it lacked moisture.
> [7]And some fell among thorns; and the thorns sprang up with it, and choked it.
> [8]And other fell on good ground, and sprang

up, and bare fruit an hundredfold. And when
he had said these things, he cried, He that
hath ears to hear, let him hear.
Luke 8:5-8, KJV

The parable starts with a sower sowing seed and verses 5 through 8 unfolds what happened when the seed was sown in four types of ground. The disciples asked Jesus to explain the parable, and He does in Luke 8:11-15. He tells them that the seed being sown is the Word of God and describes what transpired when the seed of the Word of God was heard by four groups of people. From this, we can ascertain that the seed of the Word of God is sown by speaking. Otherwise, how could the people have heard it? We sow, or plant, the seed of the Word of God by speaking.

The Word of God is a seed and it works like other seeds. It produces what it is.[18] Corn seed produces corn and apple seed produces apples. If it is healing seed (God's Word on healing), it produces healing. If it is salvation seed (God's Word on Salvation), it produces salvation. In the *"Parable of the Sower"* three groups of people did not keep the Word of God in their heart (the ground was the heart). They let the seed of the Word of God be trampled, get withered, and be choked. Because there is time between sowing a seed and seeing a harvest, you have to be active about tending to the seed of the Word of God. The Word of God is a seed and a seed has to be kept (given attention). In nature, what would happen if a farmer did not water (give attention to) his seed? That farmer would not experience a harvest from that seed. What would happen if a farmer planted a seed and then went out and dug it up? The farmer would not have a harvest. You have to keep the Word of God in your heart, because what comes forth in your life comes out of your heart. If it's not the Word of God, it will be something else.

How do we keep the Word of God in our hearts? We keep the Word of God in our hearts or planted by:

1) Hearing and hearing it which is the same way it got there initially
2) Speaking it and speaking it and speaking it.

You want to keep hearing it and speaking it until the harvest comes. Your speaking it is one way of your hearing it also. You can hear it from speaking it, and you can hear it by others speaking it. If you begin to speak something opposite of the Word of God, you are digging up the seed. You have to keep the Word of God in your heart until the harvest comes.

Not only does a seed need to stay planted, it also has to be watered. How do we water the seed of the Word of God? There is such a thing as watering by the Word of God.[19] We water the seed of the Word of God by speaking and speaking, and continuing to speak the Word of God. The fourth group heard the Word of God, got it in their hearts, kept it in their hearts and they received results in their lives. The major significance of keeping the seed of the Word of God in your heart is you will speak it out your mouth and get a harvest. What will that harvest be? That harvest will be what you are speaking. The seed produces what it is.

I Peter 1:23 is another scripture referring to the Word of God as a seed.

[23]Being born again, not of corruptible seed,
but of incorruptible, by the word of God,
which liveth and abideth for ever.
I Peter 1:23, KJV

This scripture is really good, because it also proclaims that the Word of God is "incorruptible seed." This seed does not perish. It does not decay, and it is not tainted. It does not return void, but produces exactly what it is supposed to, and the Word of God produces good things.

In Mark 4:13 Jesus enlightens his disciples about how vital the *"Parable of the Sower"* is to understand all the other parables. Jesus talks about the seed again in the *"Parable of the Growing Seed"* and describes how the Kingdom of God is like a man sowing seed.[20] We can glean four things from these two parables:

1) That the seed is the Word of God
2) That the Kingdom of God operates based on sowing seed
3) That man can sow the seed
4) That the seed is sown by speaking.

We should not be surprised that the Kingdom of God functions based on the Word of God. If you think about kings and their kingdoms throughout the history of mankind, how did they function? They functioned based on the king's word (what the king said, declared or decreed), and what the king spoke is what was done or what came to pass. The way the Kingdom of God functions is no different. God's

Kingdom functions based on speaking the King's Word. Jesus is our King and He speaks the Word of God. If we want to operate effectively in the Kingdom of God, we have to speak the King's Language which is the Word of God.

GOD'S WORD CAN MAKE YOU PROSPER AND HAVE GOOD SUCCESS

THE LORD TOLD ABRAHAM THAT HE WAS GIVING Abraham's descendants land. He chose a man named Joshua to lead the children of Israel (Abraham's descendants) into this promised land. To help equip Joshua to be successful with this assignment, the Lord tells Joshua to be strong and courageous and gave him a directive. Read something from this directive below.

> [8]This book of the law shall not depart out of
> thy mouth; but thou shalt meditate therein
> day and night, that thou mayest observe to
> do according to all that is written therein: for
> then thou shalt make thy way prosperous, and
> then thou shalt have good success.
> Joshua 1:8, KJV

THE LORD COMMANDS JOSHUA TO DO THE FOL-lowing to be prosperous and have good success:

1) Keep the Word of God in his mouth
2) Meditate on the Word of God
3) Do the Word of God.

Notice that the key to Joshua being prosperous and having good success was all associated with the Word of God. The Word of God will do the same for us. It will make us advance and have good success.

There were people with Joshua who let the Word of God depart from their mouths and they did not enter the Promised Land. Speaking that *"You can never get a promotion or a better job"* is an everyday example of letting the Word of God depart from your mouth. People speak things like this over and over because it's what they really believe, and they are seeing (having and experiencing) it in their lives. You can instead begin to meditate on the Word of God (think about yourself promoted, see yourself promoted, use a vision board if needed) and speak words that agree with the Word of God. Words from Psalm 75:7, Deuteronomy 28:13 and Joshua 1:8 are good places to start. You can speak something similar to this, *"Lord God promotion comes from you. I Thank You that I'm above only and not beneath and that I'm prosperous and have good success."*

Even before Joshua began leading the children of Israel, he was already keeping the Word of God on his lips. In the Book of Numbers, when ten of the spies spoke against having the Promised Land, Joshua did not. He kept saying what God said about the land (that they could have it). Joshua was not letting the Word of God depart from his mouth. He led the children of Israel into the Promised Land and divided to them their inheritance. He was very successful in his life. This indicates to me that he did as commanded in Joshua 1:8 and the Word caused him to be prosperous and have good success.

God's Word Is Confirmed With Signs Following

THERE ARE TIMES WHEN GOD CONFIRMS (MAKES sure, corroborates, establishes, or guarantees) His Word with signs. Mark 16:20 familiarizes us with this aspect of the Word of God (read it below).

> [20]And they went forth, and preached every where, the Lord working with them, and confirming the word with signs following. Amen.
> Mark 16:20, KJV

Definitions for the word "sign" from the Old and New Testaments include a mark, a signal, a miracle, a token, an indication of the supernatural, a wonder, or something that serves as evidence.[21] God can make sure, corroborate, establish, or guarantee His Word by showing a mark, a signal, a miracle, a token, something that indicates the supernatural, a wonder, or something that serves as evidence.

After the flood in Genesis Chapter 9, God talks to Noah about a covenant. The flood had destroyed all flesh on the earth, except for life in the ark. God promises Noah that all life on the earth would never be destroyed again by a flood. To assure Noah and creation that this would never happen again, God informs Noah that He (God) was making a sign to mark this pledge. Scriptures in Genesis 9:12-16 capture some of the pledge.

> [12]And God said, This is the token of the covenant which I make between me and you and every living creature that is with you, for perpetual generations:
> [13]I do set my bow in the cloud, and it shall be for a token of a covenant between me and the earth.
> [14]And it shall come to pass, when I bring a cloud over the earth, that the bow shall be seen in the cloud:
> [15]And I will remember my covenant, which is between me and you and every living creature of all flesh; and the waters shall no more become a flood to destroy all flesh.
> [16]And the bow shall be in the cloud; and I will look upon it, that I may remember the everlasting covenant between God and every living creature of all flesh that is upon the earth.
> Genesis 9:12-16, KJV

God made the rainbow as the sign to confirm His Word to Noah and creation that all life on the earth would never be destroyed again by a flood. Probably 100% of the people reading this book have seen a rainbow after rain. It is how God confirmed (guaranteed) this Word with a sign following.

The next example comes from the New Testament. In Luke Chapter 2 there were shepherds in the fields watching their flocks and an angel of the Lord appeared.

> [10]And the angel said unto them, Fear not: for, behold, I bring you good tidings of great joy, which shall be to all people.
> [11]For unto you is born this day in the city of David a Saviour, which is Christ the Lord.
> [12]And this shall be a sign unto you; Ye shall find the babe wrapped in swaddling clothes, lying in a manger.
> [13]And suddenly there was with the angel a multitude of the heavenly host praising God, and saying,
> [14]Glory to God in the highest, and on earth peace, good will toward men.
> [15]And it came to pass, as the angels were gone away from them into heaven, the shepherds said one to another, Let us now go even unto Bethlehem, and see this thing which is come to pass, which the Lord hath made known unto us.
> [16]And they came with haste, and found Mary, and Joseph, and the babe lying in a manger.

^{17}And when they had seen it, they made
known abroad the saying which was told
them concerning this child.
Luke 2:10-17, KJV

Jesus has been born in Bethlehem and this angel reports His birth to the shepherds. He tells them where they can find the baby and gives them a sign that would corroborate this Word that the Savior had been born. The sign was the baby would be wrapped in swaddling clothes and lying in a manger. The shepherds went to Bethlehem to see this Word of the Lord. It's awesome to read in Luke 2:16 that the shepherds went in haste. We all need to be eager to see the Word of God manifested, to see it come to pass, to see it confirmed, and to see it ratified. In Luke 2:16, the shepherds saw the sign. When they got to Bethlehem, they found the baby lying in the manger. The Word of God spoken to the shepherds was confirmed with signs following. A good reason for us to believe and speak the Word of God is because God confirms His Word with signs following.

Speaking Truth 7

God's Word Can Heal

PROVERBS 4:20-23 IS A PORTION OF SCRIPTURE that reveals that God's Word has healing power.

> [20]My son, attend to my words; incline thine
> ear unto my sayings.
> [21]Let them not depart from thine eyes; keep
> them in the midst of thine heart.
> [22]For they are life unto those that find them,
> and health to all their flesh.
> [23]Keep thy heart with all diligence; for out of
> it are the issues of life.
> Proverbs 4:20-23, KJV

Verse 22 makes it known that the Word of God is life for us, and health (medicine, a cure and healing) to our flesh.[22] The other scriptures indicate how this can happen. One way the Word of God can be life and health to all of one's flesh is by the person:

1) Giving attention to the Word of God

33

2) Listening to God's Word

3) Keeping God's Word before their eyes

4) Keeping the Word of God in the midst of their heart.

Speaking is also involved with this. Why do I say this? Because of what is written in Matthew 12:34, "For out of the abundance of the heart the mouth speaketh."[23] If you are keeping the Word of God in the midst of your heart, you will speak the Word of God out of your mouth. Hearing and hearing and hearing the Word of God will get the Word of God in the midst of your heart. What you keep in the midst of your heart will come out of your mouth and manifest in your life. Make a point to give God's Word your attention over other words. The words you give attention to will form what gets in your heart and what comes out of your mouth. You want to be like the woman with the issue of blood and keep speaking words of health and healing.

Another scripture that verifies that God's Word can heal is Psalm 107:20, which says, "He sent His word, and healed them, and delivered them from their destructions."[24] Now that we've read Psalm 107:20, consider it in relation to the account of a centurion and his servant in Matthew Chapter 8. Jesus goes to Capernaum and is made aware that the centurion has a servant at home, paralyzed. As Jesus is going to heal the servant, the centurion sent word that Jesus could just speak the word only, and his servant would be healed.[25] This man believed that Jesus could just speak the Word and his servant be healed, even with his servant not being at the same location as Jesus. After hearing this, Jesus said that the centurion had what he believed. What was it that the centurion believed? He believed that Jesus could just speak the Word and his servant would be healed. Reading Matthew 8:13 we learn that the servant was healed at the same hour that Jesus spoke the Word. Jesus did exactly what the centurion said and believed. He sent His Word and healed and delivered the centurion's servant. There was power in the WORD being spoken to heal.

Speaking Truth 8

God's Word Is A Weapon

THE BOOK OF JAMES REMINDS US IN JAMES 4:7 that we are to submit to God, resist the devil, and he will flee from us. There is an example of Jesus speaking the Word of God in Matthew 4:1-11 while resisting (standing against, withstanding and opposing) the devil.[26] Ephesians 6:17 describes the Word of God as, "The sword of the Spirit."[27] A sword is a weapon. The devil approaches Jesus after He has fasted in the wilderness. During this occurrence, the devil attempted some of the same things with Jesus that he used on Adam and Eve. He tried to get Jesus to eat something that God had not permitted Jesus to eat. Since Jesus only did what the Father said, the Father had instructed him to not eat. If Jesus had turned the stones to bread and eaten, it would have been sin for Him and He would have been separated from the Father and not able to fulfill the plan for our redemption. The devil got Adam and Eve to eat something they were not supposed to, and it resulted in sin and separation from God. It stole their position (they fell from the glory) and the relationship they once had with the Father. What did Jesus do to stop the devil from stealing His relationship with the Father

37

and His destiny? The answer is in Matthew 4:4 where Jesus said, "It is written, Man shall not live by bread alone, but by every word that proceedeth out of the mouth of God."[28] Jesus spoke the Word of God to stand against the devil.

The devil said something to Eve about dying. He did the same thing with Jesus. He told Eve that she would not die if she ate the forbidden fruit.[29] This sounds like him saying to Jesus that the angels would protect Jesus if He jumped off the temple (meaning Jesus would not die). Jesus was destined to die, but it was not this way, it was by way of the cross. Had Jesus died by jumping off the temple, He would not have fulfilled the plan for Him to be the Lamb slain for the sin of the world. What did Jesus do to stop the devil from killing Him in this manner? The answer is in Matthew 4:7 where Jesus said to the devil, "It is written again, Thou shalt not tempt the Lord thy God."[30] Jesus spoke the Word of God.

In the third temptation of Jesus, the devil tried to get Jesus to accept his kingdoms. This is similar to the devil telling Eve if she ate fruit that was forbidden, she could have something she didn't already have. He told her she could be like God if she ate the fruit. She already had this state of existence, as she was already created in God's image and likeness. The devil told Jesus he'd give Jesus kingdoms if Jesus would fall down and worship him. God had already spoken that Jesus had a Kingdom that would never end.[31] The devil was trying to get Jesus to accept his kingdoms, thus destroying Jesus' destiny in the Kingdom God had for Him. What did Jesus do to stop the devil from destroying something in His life? Once again, in Matthew 4:10, Jesus spoke the Word of God. After Jesus spoke the Word of God to stand against, resist, and oppose the devil, the devil left. When anything attempts theft, death, or destruction in your life, one of your weapons is speaking the Word of God.

We have just read powerful truths about the Word of God. Section Two contains Speaking Truths about the role of our own words in determining what we see (have and experience) in our lives. As you read Section Two, meditate on the benefits of speaking God's Word. This WORD that, is a creative force, God confirms with signs following, does not return void, produces faith, is incorruptible seed, is how the Kingdom of God functions, can make you prosper and have good success, has the power to heal, and can protect.

SECTION TWO

SPEAKING TRUTHS
ABOUT YOUR WORDS

THE PURPOSE OF SPEAKING IS TO PRODUCE A result. You read about how God speaks to produce results in Section One, the same is also true for mankind. God gave mankind speaking ability with power to accomplish things. We can discern this from what Jesus said in Matthew 12:36: "But I say unto you, That every idle word that men shall speak, they shall give account thereof in the day of judgment."[32] This reveals that the Lord expects us to speak words that accomplish something.

As kings and priests unto God the Father, we want to walk more in this spiritual truth about speaking. Part of our kingship is decreeing a thing that it be established. Throughout history when a king decreed a thing, it was so. To be more effective for the Kingdom of God, God's children must speak words with the deliberate intention of producing something for the Kingdom. We should all also want to see (have and experience) the blessing that Jesus has made available for us, through His redemptive works.

This section of the book will focus on man's words, and the importance of speaking the Word of God, so that we see what God desires for the Church and our lives. There are 11 Speaking Truths in this section.

SPEAKING TRUTH 9

YOUR WORDS HAVE POWER

GOD'S SPEAKING HAS POWER, AND SO DOES MAN'S. Proverbs 18:21 states that "Death and life are in the power of the tongue."[33] From this scripture, and others, we will learn that man's words have power. This Speaking Truth will start with the account of the people who were building the Tower of Babel. In this account, there is a connection between the people's speaking, the power of agreement and what they were able to accomplish.

The people building the tower were in such agreement from speaking the same thing that the Lord said in Genesis 11:6, "Behold, they are one people, and they all have the same language. And this is what they began to do, and now nothing which they purpose to do will be impossible for them."[34] Why was it that nothing this group of people planned to do would be impossible? The Lord gave the answer in Genesis 11:7 when He said, "Let us go down, and there confound their language, that they may not understand one another's speech."[35] It was because of their speaking the same thing that nothing would be impossible for them. Something happening to their speaking was the answer to stopping them.

These people were operating in tremendous power, and that power was connected to their words. This also demonstrates that believing and speaking the same thing gets you into agreement. They were all in agreement about getting the tower built, but once something happened to their speech the building stopped. Something else is important here; what these people were saying was so powerful that it (their speaking) would have accomplished something that God did not will to happen. The Lord had told them to fill the earth and they were trying to leave the earth and build a tower to the heavens. Their words were making the Word of the Lord for them to fill the earth of no effect in their lives.

The thing that stopped these people from having the will of God was what they were saying. The same can keep us from experiencing the will of God in our lives. The Lord did not say He was going down to stop their imagination, their agreement, or their work. He went down to do something about their speaking. Once something happened to their speaking, they were able to experience the will of God for their lives and go throughout the earth, filling it as God had desired for them all along. If what you are saying is not the Word of God, change your speaking. Your words carry power. Began to speak the Word of God so that you see (have and experience) what God wills for your life.

For the next example of the power of words, let's return to passages from the Books of Exodus and Numbers. The Lord communicates to Moses that He's delivering the children of Israel from slavery, and giving them land. This land, however, was inhabited by other people. Moses sent 12 men (one from

Your Words Have Power

each of the tribes of Israel) to spy out the land for 40 days and bring back word.

The spies reported that the land flowed with milk and honey (as the Lord had said) and showed the people fruit from the land. As you read Numbers Chapter 13, it's apparent that there is a difference between what two of the spies said about the land and possessing it compared to the other ten. Joshua and Caleb spoke that the Lord had given them the land, and they were able to have possession of it. The other ten spies focused more on the inhabitants of the land, and reported that they were not able to have the land. The Word of God referred to their report as a bad and evil report. Most of the people believed the bad report of the ten spies more than the Word of God that He had given them the land.

Hearing the bad report was so devasting that the people wished they had stayed in Egypt or would just die in the wilderness. The report that the ten spies gave was not good news. The people heard the bad report ten times more than the good news that God had given them the land. The bad report was being magnified more than the promise of God's Word. It matters greatly what you hear. After all the miracles, signs, and wonders, that the children of Israel had witnessed they now believed because of what the ten spies spoke that God could not give them the land He promised. This illustrates the power of words. What these people heard the most got in their hearts in abundance and formed what they believed and what they spoke.

The people did not receive the Word of the Lord and spoke of dying in the wilderness. The Lord heard how the people were speaking and said it would happen to them, just as they had spoken.[36] The ten spies and all of the people who were 20 years and older (with the exception of Joshua and Caleb) died in the wilderness and did not enter the Promised Land. They experienced both of the things they had spoken (death in the wilderness and not being able to enter the Promised Land). The power of death and life was in their tongue. Joshua and Caleb, however, said what God said. They spoke the promise of God to have the land regardless of the cities being fortified, who lived there, and of what the giants looked like. Joshua and Caleb kept speaking the Word of God, and they experienced life in the Promised Land. They did not magnify the bad report. They did not focus on the bad report. They focused on the promise of God and kept speaking the promise of God and entered the Promised Land.

Your Words Can Make Things Change

WORDS ARE AFFECTING YOUR EVERYDAY LIFE, and your entire existence. Think of how believing in your heart and confessing with your mouth that Jesus is the Son of God, that Jesus died and paid the price for your sins, and that God raised Him from the dead CHANGED your life. Likewise, believing in your heart and speaking words can change other things about your life.

The Lord appeared to a man named Abram in Genesis Chapter 12 and tells him that He is going to make him a nation and give his descendants land. When the Lord told Abram this, Abram was old, and his wife was old and barren, and they did not have a child. Three chapters later, in Genesis 15:2, Abram is still referring to himself as childless. He is not speaking about himself, what God had said about him (that he was a nation). In order for Abram to get to nation status, he had to have a child. Given Abram's age, and that of his wife and her barrenness, it was impossible for them to have a child and become this great nation. Yes, it was impossible for them alone, but with God all things are possible, and God had come on the scene and spoke a WORD for this situation. We read about how God confirms His Word with signs following in Speaking Truth #6. For God to perform this WORD in Abram's life, Abram is going to have to change what he is saying. To assist Abram with speaking the right words, the Lord instructs him to change his name to Abraham, which meant father of a multitude.[37]

Abram changes his name and when he does it results in him now saying what God said about him, instead of continuing to say he's someone without an heir. He's now calling himself "a father of a multitude" every time he says his name. He's saying this, although Isaac (the son of promise) is not yet born. He's saying this when his wife is still old and barren. Whenever Abraham says his name, he's now speaking the Word of God. When we know God's will for our lives, we are to begin saying those things about ourselves and for our lives. We are to speak God's Word. We are to say what God says about us and what God says is for us. After Abraham changed what he was saying about himself, things changed. His son Isaac was born. What God says about you is the truth, and if you believe it and speak it, it will come to pass.

Many are familiar with the account of David and Goliath in the Book of I Samuel Chapter 17. The armies of the Philistines and Israel were gathered for battle. The Philistines had a champion warrior named Goliath who was over nine feet tall and had been a warrior from his youth. Goliath insisted that one man from each nation fight instead of the entire armies. The army of the man who won would be deemed victorious. Goliath had come out morning and evening for 40 days terrorizing Israel over this.

David, a young Hebrew shepherd, was sent to take food to the battle area and report back to his father about his brothers. Once there, David heard Goliath taunting Israel. David was not a war champion like Goliath, but Goliath's treatment of God's covenant people was unacceptable to him. He made this statement about Goliath in I Samuel 17:26, "For who is this uncircumcised Philistine that he should defy the armies of the living God?"[38] The sign of the people who God had covenant with was circumcision.[39] People who did not have this covenant with God were referred to as the "uncircumcised." David not only knew about Israel's covenant with God, he believed in the covenant and brought it to remembrance when he called Goliath "uncircumcised." As Abraham's descendants, the children of Israel were supposed to defeat their enemies. With the covenant promises in his heart David agreed to fight on behalf of Israel. David recounts to King Saul how the LORD had delivered him from a lion and a bear and said that the Lord would also deliver him from Goliath.

When Goliath notices who would challenge him, he mocks and curses David. Read how David responded.

> [45]Then said David to the Philistine, Thou comest to me with a sword, and with a spear, and with a shield: but I come to thee in the name of the LORD of hosts, the God of the armies of Israel, whom thou hast defied. [46]This day will the LORD deliver thee into mine hand; and I will smite thee, and take

thine head from thee; and I will give the car-
cases of the host of the Philistines this day
unto the fowls of the air, and to the wild
beasts of the earth; that all the earth may
know that there is a God in Israel.
I Samuel 17:45-46, KJV

David ran toward Goliath and defeated him. I Samuel 17:48-54 details how everything happened, just as David spoke. It seems no one from Israel was willing to respond to Goliath's challenge until David came on the scene. Goliath spoke words, taunting Israel morning and evening for 40 days. David showed up and started speaking about Israel's covenant, how the Lord had delivered him from a lion and bear, and about the Name of the Lord and things changed. What had been happening for 40 days changed. Things can be changed by speaking the right words.

For the third example we will revisit scriptures from Matthew Chapter 9 and Mark Chapter 5 related to the woman who had the blood condition for 12 years. The woman had gone to many physicians and spent all her money but had only gotten worse. The woman was saying, "If I only touch His garment, I will get well."[40] She spoke of healing. She kept speaking of healing. She even spoke it to herself. What would have happened if this woman had been going around saying (even saying to herself), "*I know even if I touch the hem of His garment, I will not get well.*" She would not have seen healing, even though healing was in His garment. The woman had to say the right thing to change this condition in her life.

If the woman had been saying, "*If I touch his garment I'll be healed*" one week and saying "*I'm going to touch his garment but I don't' think I'll be healed*" the next week, she would have been digging up her seed. This would have also indicated that she was not in faith. She did not really believe she would be healed. She was not convinced she would be healed. She was not truly expecting to be healed. She would have been engaging in what is taught in James 1:6. She would have been wavering and not able to receive. Thank God, she had heard of Jesus and healing. She heard the Word of God and she spoke healing and only healing. She held fast to her confession and she saw healing in her life. Words are seeds, and seeds take time to produce. A farmer does not plant a seed and see a harvest in five days. Keep watering the seed by holding fast to your confession of the Word of God until the harvest comes (until you see what you are saying). Her testimony is in the Word of God, so that we can learn from it. She spoke healing, and she kept speaking healing, and she saw the blood condition of 12 years change. If you want to see something change, speak what you want to see. Speak what God's Word says belongs to you.

To end this Speaking Truth we'll review how speaking words have a role in the ultimate life-changing experience of being born again.

> [9]That if thou shalt confess with thy mouth
> the Lord Jesus, and shalt believe in thine
> heart that God hath raised him from the
> dead, thou shalt be saved.
> [10]For with the heart man believeth unto

righteousness; and with the mouth confession is made unto salvation.
Romans 10:9-10, KJV

It's the believing and the speaking that leads to salvation. How many of you know, when you got born again, you
CHANGED. According to II Corinthians 5:17 you became
a new creation in Christ. Your heart becomes different when
you get born again. This change occurs because you believe
in your heart and confess (speak) with your mouth the Lord
Jesus Christ and that God raised Him from the dead. Words
are a part of you experiencing the glorious CHANGE of
salvation.

WORDS CAN ACTIVATE THE BLESSING

JAMES 3:10 STIPULATES THAT WE SHOULD NOT have blessing and cursing coming out of the same mouth. This indicates that speaking is connected to the blessing and the curse. This Speaking Truth will examine how words are associated with the blessing.

The blessing is introduced in Genesis 1:28, when God blessed Adam and Eve. God blessed Adam and Eve by saying something. The blessing came by God pronouncing or speaking it. One definition for the word "blessing" in Genesis 1:28 is "An act of God that is a benefit to man."[41] The word advantage is a synonym for the word benefit.[42] We can think of the blessing as an empowerment from God that gives man an advantage to do something or have something.

God spoke the blessing in Genesis 1:28 on the lives of Adam and Eve, to achieve desirable outcomes. Some of those desirable outcomes included being fruitful and multiplying, filling the earth, subduing the earth, and having dominion over all the works of His hand.[43] God blessed Adam and Eve to accomplish these outcomes by pronouncing this blessing on their lives.

The blessing was not only spoken for the lives of Adam and Eve. The Lord spoke the blessing for Noah and his family, for Abraham and for Isaac.[44] Why could the blessing be spoken for the lives of Noah, Abraham, and Isaac after being spoken for Adam and Eve? That blessing could be spoken for their lives, because when God spoke the blessing for Adam and Eve, He was pronouncing the blessing for all of mankind. All of mankind was in Adam and Eve.

We've looked at Adam and Eve, now let's read a few other places where words are linked to the blessing. In Genesis Chapter 12, the Lord blessed Abram the same way He blessed Adam and Eve. The Lord blessed Abram by pronouncing the blessing on Abram's life. Read Genesis 12:2-3 to learn the planned outcomes of this blessing. In Genesis Chapter 14 Abram and his men defeated four kings and saved his nephew, Lot. Five other kings and their men had attempted to defeat these four kings, but could not. The blessing gave Abram and his men an advantage for battle. Why am I writing it was the blessing? Because Melchizedek attributes Abram's victory to it in Genesis 14:19-20. Abram's rescue of his nephew, Lot, and his family indicates that others can experience benefits from the blessing on you. Again, how did this blessing get on Abram's life? The Lord spoke it.

After Abraham's death, the Lord spoke the blessing on the life of Isaac. Genesis Chapter 27 has the account of Isaac speaking the blessing on the life of his son Jacob. Esau and Jacob were the twin sons of Isaac. Esau was the firstborn and expecting the blessing. However, Isaac spoke the blessing on the life of Jacob. When Esau came to receive the blessing, Isaac informed him that the blessing had already been given to Jacob. How did Isaac give Jacob the blessing? The answer is in Genesis 27:27-29, where Isaac blessed Jacob by saying something. Isaac pronounced the blessing on the life of Jacob by speaking words.

The encounter between Esau and his father, Isaac, described in Genesis 27:34-38, portrays how real the blessing is. Take the time to read the reaction of Esau when he learned that his father had already spoken the blessing on Jacob's life. Isaac asserts that he has blessed Jacob and that Jacob will indeed be blessed. All Isaac had done was speak the blessing to activate it on Jacob's life, and he decreed with certainty that the blessing would produce. In Genesis Chapter 48 Jacob speaks the blessing on his two grandsons (Ephraim and Manasseh). There is a pattern of speaking the blessing.

There is a connection between words and the blessing of the tithe. The Lord informs the children of Israel in Malachi Chapter 3 that the windows of heaven would be opened to pour out blessing for them and that the devour would be rebuked for their sakes if they brought Him the whole tithe. Malachi 3:13-14 highlights for us that words can hinder the blessing of the tithe. Right after the Lord reminds His people about the blessing of the tithe He starts talking about their words. He mentions that they had spoken harshly against Him. He heard them complaining about serving Him and saying keeping God's commandments was useless. Deuteronomy Chapter 26 also contains information indicating that words are connected to the tithe. In this chapter, the Lord tells the children of Israel what to say when they bring the tithe.

One can bring the tithe and there is a blessing with the tithe, but believing and speaking things similar to these will hinder the blessing of the tithe, "*I'll never get ahead; We're never going to have anything; I always have more month than money; or I'm tithing but the windows of heaven aren't pouring me out anything.*" Make it a lifestyle to not speak against the blessing of the tithe. Speak what the Word of God says about the tithe. It will build your faith in what God says about the tithe, and will keep your angels working to bring that WORD to pass for you.

There is an account of Jesus speaking the blessing in Luke 9:16. When He does the multiplication feature of the blessing manifests. Luke 9:10-17 records the account of Jesus feeding a multitude of people that consisted of at least 5,000 men. Jesus taught and healed people, and afterwards the disciples wanted to send them to surrounding towns to obtain lodging and food. Jesus, however, instructed them to feed the people instead. The disciples expressed that there was only two fish and five loaves, which was not enough to feed everyone. Jesus had the disciples organize the people into groups and scripture says the following in Luke 9:16-17 about what happened.

> [16]Then he took the five loaves and the two
> fishes, and looking up to heaven, he blessed
> them, and brake, and gave to the disciples to
> set before the multitude.
> [17]And they did eat, and were all filled:
> and there was taken up of fragments that
> remained to them twelve baskets.
> Luke 9:16-17, KJV

The word "blessed" in verse 16 is the Greek word "eulogēsen," which means "to speak well of."[45] Jesus caused the blessing to be activated on the two fish and five loaves by speaking, and notice He had to be speaking well of things. Speaking words of the curse is not speaking well of things. Jesus spoke the blessing and the fish and loaves multiplied. It is common to read about increase with the blessing.[46]

For this Speaking Truth we have seen God speak the blessing, Jesus speak the blessing, and people speak the blessing. The blessing was activated in all of these instances by speaking words. Galatians 3:13-14 says that Christ redeemed us from the curse of the law so that we could have the blessing of Abraham. As mentioned in the Introduction, the Christian is to be saying the things of their redemption and the blessing is a part of our redemption. We are to be speaking words of the blessing. Another scripture that corroborates that the blessing is invoked by speaking is Isaiah 65:16.

> [16]So [it shall be] that he who invokes a
> blessing on himself in the land shall do so
> by saying, May the God of truth *and* fidelity
> [the Amen] bless me;...
> Isaiah 65:16, AMPC

Notice from this scripture that one who invokes (puts into effect or operation) a blessing does so by saying something.

YOUR WORDS CAN CAUSE ANGELS TO WORK ON YOUR BEHALF

THERE ARE PASSAGES IN THE WORD OF GOD about angels bringing people messages, battling, being involved with healing, and providing protection. Psalm 103:20 provides insight about how angels function.

> [20]Bless the LORD, ye his angels, that excel in strength, that do his commandments, hearkening unto the voice of his word.
> Psalm 103:20, KJV

Psalm 103:20 illuminates for us that angels accomplish, bring forth, bring to pass, and perform the Lord's Word.[47] The verse reveals something that can cause angels to do this. It highlights how angels listen to and obey the voice that speaks the Lord's Word. If one reads the verse too quickly, they may think it says that angels only heed the voice of the Lord. Yes, angels do heed the voice of the Lord, but this scripture is saying that angels heed any voice that speaks God's

Word. We can also conclude from this scripture that these angels do not obey the voice that is not speaking the Lord's Word. There is another angel who listens to bring forth, bring to pass, and perform words. Satan listens for words that are opposite the Word of God and that are words of the curse to bring them to pass.

For this Speaking Truth we'll start with scripture in Daniel Chapter 10 where Daniel has a vision and an angel appears to him.

> ¹²Then said he unto me, Fear not, Daniel: for
> from the first day that thou didst set thine
> heart to understand, and to chasten thyself
> before thy God, thy words were heard, and I
> am come for thy words.
> Daniel 10:12, KJV

The angel appears to Daniel and tells him that his words were heard and that he had come in response to Daniel's words. The angel came because of Daniel's words. The angel then explains to Daniel some things about the vision.

The second example is from Acts Chapter 10 where an angel was involved in the account of the first Gentile who became born again. An angel comes to a man named Cornelius and tells him that his prayers and his giving had come up before God. The angel instructs Cornelius to send for Peter, which he does. Meanwhile, Peter has a vision and the Holy Spirit informs him that men are coming. The angel came as a result of the words Cornelius was praying and it led to Cornelius and those with him being the first Gentiles born again and filled with the Holy Spirit. Read all of Acts Chapter 10 to learn more about this fascinating encounter.

Another place in scripture where an angel brings forth something because of a person's words is in Luke Chapter One. A priest named Zacharias was serving in the temple. Zacharias was old, and he and his wife Elizabeth (who was not only old, but also barren) had no children. An angel appeared to Zacharias and tells him that his prayer had been heard. This is similar to what happened to Daniel. Are you beginning to see a pattern with the angels saying something to people about their words being heard?

The angel exposes for us what Zacharias had been praying when he announces that Zacharias and his wife would have a son. Zacharias was praying words that agreed with the Word of God. God's will for the children of Israel was that there be none barren among them.[48] The angel commands Zacharias to name the baby John and tells him things about his son's life (which included that he would prepare the people for the Lord). This child was *John the Baptist.* The angel came because of Zacharias' words that he prayed, and Zacharias and his wife had a son. These angels do not respond to just any words, they respond to words that are the Word of the Lord and agree with the Word of the Lord.

The Bible states that children have angels and that angels have been sent to provide aid and services for believers.[49] Not only should we know about angels and their availability for us, we should be teaching our children at home and in Children's Churches about how to activate their angels. You can teach them to say daily and definitely in the time of any trouble, *"Thank You Lord that you have given angels charge over me and they protect me and keep me safe day and night."* There are angels available to us and to get these angels to accomplish things, bring forth things and perform on our behalf we are to speak the right words. We don't have to wonder or attempt to guess what the right words are. Thank God He told us in Psalm 103:20 that these angels listen to and obey the voice that speaks the Lord's Word.

Your Words Tell You What You Believe and are an Indicator of Your Faith

THERE IS A SPIRITUAL TRUTH IN LUKE 6:45 AND Matthew 12:34 that's important to become familiar with. This spiritual truth is that we speak what is in our hearts in abundance.

> [45]A good man out of the good treasure of his heart bringeth forth that which is good; and an evil man out of the evil treasure of his heart bringeth forth that which is evil: for of the abundance of the heart his mouth speaketh.
> Luke 6:45, KJV

> [34]O generation of vipers, how can ye, being evil, speak good things? for out of the abundance of the heart the mouth speaketh.
> Matthew 12:34, KJV

Romans 10:10 expresses that man believes with the heart. We just read in the two scriptures above that what's in our hearts in abundance comes out of our mouths. So, our mouths tell us what's in our heart (what it is that we believe and are convinced of). This is also confirmed by II Corinthians 4:13 which says, "I believed, and therefore have I spoken."[50]

Now, let's examine how this is all associated with what we see in our lives. Read Proverbs 4:23 below.

> [23]Keep thy heart with all diligence; for out of
> it are the issues of life.
> Proverbs 4:23, KJV

Proverbs 4:23 commands us to diligently guard our hearts, because out of our hearts is what comes forth in our lives. How does what's in our hearts come forth in our lives? It comes into our lives through our words (remember we speak what is in our hearts). The word for "issues" in Proverbs 4:23 means "boundary or border."[51] What is in your heart sets the boundaries for what can come forth in your life. Since your words come out of your heart it is then your words that set these boundaries. Your life will not go beyond the boundaries of your words. Boundaries are indicators of where something stops. If your words don't go beyond sickness to health, then your life doesn't go beyond sickness to health. Your life stops at the boundary of sickness. If your words don't go beyond poverty to prosperity, and more than enough, then your life stays at the boundary of poverty or lack. If your words don't go to confessing Jesus as Savior, then you don't get to salvation. Your life stops short of salvation. In the world there are times when you can get access to go beyond a boundary. An example of this is a passport. Your words are the passport that can expand your boundary, and believing and speaking the Word of God will exceedingly abundantly expand your boundary.

For this Speaking Truth, we need to also examine how things can get in our hearts. Things can get in our hearts through words.[52] Both the words that you speak and the words that you hear others speak can go into your heart and form what you believe. The Word of God gets in your heart as you hear it and hear it and you develop faith in it. Other words get in your heart the same way, by hearing and hearing and hearing them. We had an illustration of this in Speaking Truth #9 with the children of Israel and the ten spies in the wilderness. The ten spies spoke words that were opposite the Word of God and these words got in the hearts of the people and caused them to speak of wanting to return to Egypt or die in the wilderness.

You know the first thing that Satan did to Eve was steal the Word from her. He showed up in the garden, speaking to Eve about what the Lord God had said about the tree of the knowledge of good and evil. Eve conversates with the devil, and then he changes what God had said in Genesis 2:17. He told Eve she would not surely die if she ate of the forbidden tree. The Word of God that Eve had heard indicating that if they ate of that tree, they would surely die was now stolen from her and replaced with something else. Eve is hearing something different from what the Lord God had said (it matters what you hear). Satan showed up and the first thing he did to Eve was steal the Word of God. The Parable of the

Sower teaches that he will do this. In Speaking Truth #8 you read about Satan attempting the same thing with Jesus that he did with Eve, but Jesus held fast to the Word of God. What Eve heard impacted her life. This is why we must control what we hear, because it's through hearing that things can get in our hearts. What's in our hearts in abundance we speak forth into our lives.

How do your words indicate your faith? Matthew 11:22-24 has something that Jesus taught about faith.

> ²²And Jesus answering saith unto them, Have faith in God.
> ²³For verily I say unto you, That whosoever shall say unto this mountain, Be thou removed, and be thou cast into the sea; and shall not doubt in his heart, but shall believe that those things which he saith shall come to pass; he shall have whatsoever he saith.
> ²⁴Therefore I say unto you, What things soever ye desire, when ye pray, believe that ye receive them, and ye shall have them.
> Mark 11:22-24, KJV

In this teaching about faith, Jesus highlights the speaking and believing. Saying is mentioned three times and believing is mentioned twice. When it comes to faith *the saying part* is very important. Faith speaks what it believes. Romans 10:6 confirms that faith speaks.

> ⁶But the righteousness which is of faith spea-
> keth on this wise, Say not in thine heart,
> Who shall ascend into heaven? (that is, to
> bring Christ down from above:)
> ⁷Or, Who shall descend into the deep? (that
> is, to bring up Christ again from the dead.)
> ⁸But what saith it? The word is nigh thee,
> even in thy mouth, and in thy heart: that is,
> the word of faith, which we preach;
> Romans 10:6-8, KJV

Romans 10:8 acquaints us with what faith speaks. Faith speaks the Word of God. Verse 6 tells us what faith does not speak. Faith does not speak something that is contrary to the Word of God. Faith would not say that Jesus is coming down to go to the cross and descend gain. To speak this would be speaking against the Word of God, which teaches that Jesus has already done these things. You can identify your faith by what you are speaking, and faith does not speak against the Word of God.

In the Gospels, on several occasions, Jesus said something to people about their faith. There are times when He made statements to the people and listened to what they said. Jesus knew some of them were in faith, or what they believed by what came out of their mouths. There are two affirmations of this in this Speaking Truth.

As Jesus went to the region of Tyre and Sidon, a Canaanite woman called Him "Son of David" and asked Him to have mercy on her and deliver her daughter.⁵³ Mark 7:25 says that the woman had heard of Jesus. What she heard resulted in her asking Him to have mercy on her. Jesus said it was not proper to give children's food to dogs. In saying this, Jesus was expressing that He was sent to bring deliverance to the Jews first.[54] The woman responded by saying, "Truth, Lord: yet the dogs eat of the crumbs which fall from their masters' table."[55] Jesus announced that the woman had great faith and that she had what she desired. Jesus proclaims this woman's great faith after he heard what she said. Mark Chapter 7 also has this event recorded and it specifically indicates in Mark 7:29 that the woman's daughter was delivered because of the woman's words. Her speaking was an indicator of her faith.

Jesus says something about the centurion's faith in Matthew Chapter 8. Jewish elders reported to Jesus that the centurion had a servant at home paralyzed and he wanted Jesus to come and heal him. Jesus started for the home to heal the servant, but the centurion sent friends who reported to Jesus that the centurion had said there was no reason to come to his home but that Jesus could just speak the WORD and his servant would be healed. After Jesus heard this reported, He pronounced that He had not found anyone in Israel with such great faith as the centurion.[56] How did Jesus know the centurion had great faith? Matthew 8:9-10 provides the answer. Jesus said the centurion had great faith after Jesus heard about what the centurion said about authority and that Jesus could speak the WORD only, and his servant would be healed.

If you want to know what is in your heart in abundance listen to what you are saying over and over. Anyone can say something a few times and it not be in their heart. But, if you continue to say it over and over all the time, it will get in your heart in abundance. Let's be thankful to God that He created us to know when we are in faith (what it is we are convinced of). It's great that our words can tell us when we are in faith and when we are not. If we are not in faith, we can make changes. We can begin to hear and hear and hear the Word of God so that it gets in our hearts in abundance. As we believe and speak it, we can expect to see (have and experience) it in our lives.

YOUR WORDS DETERMINE THE DIRECTION OF YOUR LIFE

THE INTRODUCTION PROVIDED SOME INFORMA-
tion related to this Speaking Truth. From James 3:5 we
became familiar with how a man's tongue works to deter-
mine the way (the path, the course or the direction) his life
proceeds, the same way a bit does for a horse and a rudder
for a ship. We are to purposely use our words to influence the
paths our lives take. There are three references from scripture
for this Speaking Truth.

The account of the life of Samson is in Judges Chapters
13 through 16. Samson was called of God, and part of that
call was to destroy Israel's enemies. The Spirit of the Lord
would come upon Samson and give him enormous supernatural strength, but Samson had to maintain a command of the
Lord to not cut his hair to continue in this anointing. This
strength was evident when he killed a lion without a weapon
and when he destroyed 1,000 men with the jawbone of a
donkey. Samson's various acts of destroying Israel's enemies
made them determined to discover the key to his enormous

strength. He became involved with a woman named Delilah and she was tasked with finding out the secret.

Delilah asked Samson several times to tell her the secret to his strength, but initially he did not tell her the truth. After Delilah's continual nagging, Samson eventually tells her the truth and his words changed the course his life took. The incident of Samson telling Delilah the truth is described in Judges 16:16-17.

> [16]And it came to pass, when she pressed him daily with her words, and urged him, so that his soul was vexed unto death;
> [17]That he told her all his heart, and said unto her, There hath not come a razor upon mine head; for I have been a Nazarite unto God from my mother's womb: if I be shaven, then my strength will go from me, and I shall become weak, and be like any other man.
> Judges 16:16-17, KJV

When Samson told Delilah the truth about the secret to his strength, verse 17 says, "He told her all his heart." Those other times when she asked, Samson just said things to answer her. This time, when he spoke, he spoke from his heart and it changed the course that his life took from that point. Instead of Samson continuing to operate in enormous supernatural strength and defeat Israel's enemies, his words led to him now being captured, made blind and in-prisoned. The direction of his life changed once he spoke from his heart.

The Philistines were celebrating and wanted Samson to be brought from the prison as entertainment for them. During the festivities Samson says, "O Lord GOD, please remember me and please strengthen me just this time, O God, that I may at once be avenged of the Philistines for my two eyes."[57] The supernatural strength manifested and Samson destroyed more of Israel's enemies in this one action than he had in all of his other defeats of them combined. Samson died in this event, also. Dying was in Samson's heart, and he spoke it with his mouth. He said he wanted to die with the Philistines and that is what he experienced.[58] The power of death and life was in his tongue.

Mark 10:46-52 has one of the accounts in the Gospels about the healing of a blind man named Bartimaeus. As Jesus and others were going out of Jericho, Bartimaeus called out saying, "Jesus, thou son of David, have mercy on me."[59] There is something noteworthy about Bartimaeus calling Jesus "Son of David." Nathan, the Prophet, had prophesied that David would have one from his House (family) who would have a kingdom that would last forever.[60] Nathan was prophesying about the Messiah and the Jews were expecting the Messiah to be of the House of King David. Bartimaeus believed that Jesus was the Messiah of the House of David and referred to Jesus as such.

People told Bartimaeus to be quiet, but Bartimaeus cried out all the more. Bartimaeus' saying something caused something to happen. Bartimaeus' calling Jesus, "Son of David" caused Jesus to stop, pay attention to him, and ask what he wanted. Bartimaeus answered to receive his sight. It was prophesied by Isaiah that the Messiah would give sight to the blind. I believe Bartimaeus had heard this prophesy about the coming Messiah and had possibly heard about Jesus healing the blind. Bartimaeus believed that Jesus was the Messiah and spoke it. I imagine Bartimaeus believing, "*Jesus, you are the Messiah and you have sight to give to the blind and I'm ready to receive it.*" Bartimaeus' calling out for Jesus and saying it all the more led to him getting his sight and it changed the path of his life. How many of you think that Bartimaeus' life as a man with sight was different from his life as a blind man? If you want something God has said is for you, call for it and keep calling, keep speaking and keep saying until you see it. If you are not pleased with life and seeing many good days examine your believing and speaking and begin speaking what the Word of God says is for you, and change the direction of your life.

Your Words Can be Sharp, Bitter and Harsh

There are scriptures in the word of god that indicate that your words can be sharp, bitter, or harsh. These words can be sharp, bitter, and harsh to others and to yourself. Proverbs 15:1 says, "A gentle answer turns away wrath, But a harsh word stirs up anger."[61] Harsh, bitter or sharp words spoken have led to such things as friendships ending, dreams destroyed, divorce, hurt feelings, wars, people losing a job, family quarrels, and people being killed to name a few. Psalm 64:3 depicts how the tongue can be like a sword and cruel words like arrows. Think of the destruction and harm that a sword and arrows can cause. Words have the same capability. we are, therefore, to be very selective in what we speak.

Anyone who has a position in a child's life should not speak sharp, bitter, and harsh words to or about those children. We should only use our words to speak good and things of the blessing to, over, and about them. Our words should build in them the image that God has of them. Words should be spoken that lead them to believe that they are who God says they are and that they can be all that God created and purposed them to be.

Speaking sharp, bitter, harsh, and negative words over and to children can create low self-esteem and rob them of vision and desire to achieve. God made us to have vision, to build in us desire to put our hands to work towards accomplishing things. Low self-esteem can cause people to not develop their gifts, talents, and abilities that God has given them. Words go down into their hearts and as they think in their hearts is what they become.[62] Purposely speak words of faith to children that substantiate that they can have all that Jesus paid for them to have in their lives. Speak words that cause them to know that God has put His Spirit in them, that they are precious in God's sight, and God has an awesome plan and purpose for their lives that He will help them to achieve. Let's speak the blessing on the lives of children.

YOUR WORDS CAN KEEP YOU SAFE

THE WORD OF GOD PROVIDES SCRIPTURES TO help us understand that there is a relationship between our words and our safety. Proverbs 13:3 is one such scripture and it says, "He that keepeth his mouth keepeth his life: but he that openeth wide his lips shall have destruction."[63]

Psalm 91:1 discloses that the Most High has a place of safety and protection for us. Psalm 91:2 imparts that the Lord is a refuge from danger and a defense. This verse also gives instruction on how to get into this place of safety and protection. It tells us that we are to say something. It even tells us what to say (that the Lord is our refuge and fortress and that we trust in Him). The rest of Psalm 91 lists several things and circumstances that we can be safe and protected from. The Lord can be a refuge, a fortress, a defense and a protector from destruction, evil, pestilence, terrorism, weapons, plagues, accidents, trouble, and short life.[64] As we believe Psalm 91 in our hearts, and speak it, we can expect to be protected (take the time to read all of Psalm 91). We have been made aware from Psalm 91:2 that our speaking matters when it comes to this protection and safety. We should not be speaking things of calamity and harm, and expect this protection to work.

David spoke the Name of the Lord and it provided a place of safety for him. Proverbs 18:10 tells us that the Name of the Lord is a strong tower that the righteous can run to and be secure and set inaccessibly on high.[65] You can use the Name of Jesus that is above every name and it will put you above every situation or thing that can be named. This was shown by David, in I Samuel 17:45, when he said to Goliath, "But I come to thee in the name of the LORD of hosts, the God of the armies of Israel, whom thou hast defied."[66] David ran toward Goliath with the Name of the Lord on his lips (being a strong tower and place of safety for him) and it put him outside the reach of the enemy. If you are set *inaccessibly on high*, you are not only above things, you are outside of their reach. Psalm 91:7 says something similar, "But it shall not come nigh thee."[67] Believing and saying the Lord is your defender, shelter, safety, and protector can keep you from being harmed, even when harm is all around.

David went towards Goliath with the Name of the Lord being a refuge and fortress and Goliath could not destroy him. There is no indication that Goliath did anything to David. Goliath came toward David with his natural weapons (a sword, a spear, and a javelin). David had natural items also (his slingshot and stones). However, in addition to those, he came with the supernatural Name of the Lord. When something comes against you, use the supernatural Name of the Lord Jesus. Using the Name of the Lord Jesus is done by speaking. Now, if David had been saying, *"I'm going in the Name of the Lord, but I don't know, this guy is huge and has been defeating people since his youth,"* David would have been revealing to us that he believed more in Goliath's ability than in the Word of God. These things about Goliath were facts, but David had to believe more in the Name of the Lord and the covenant that Israel had with God. This is what David did. He believed in and spoke about the Name of the Lord and Israel's covenant, and spoke that the Philistine was going to be defeated just like the lion and the bear. Did you notice David didn't speak about Goliath's size, Goliath's age, or Goliath's war victories. He just spoke about His God, what his God had done in his life, and what was going to happen to Goliath and the rest of the Philistines that day. David also had not been listening to Goliath for 40 days. He'd been somewhere, shepherding the sheep and meditating on the Word of God. He had to have already been hearing the Word of God. He showed up full of the Word of God with the Word of God in his heart and coming out of his mouth. He'd been somewhere, giving attention to the WORD.

Another example of words having a role in someone's safety is in Acts Chapter 27, where the Apostle Paul spoke words about his life and the life of all the men on a ship with him sailing to Rome. At one point during the voyage, Paul perceived that there was impending danger and warns the men. The centurion was persuaded by others and chose to continue the journey. A vicious storm arose that made the men lose all hope of surviving.

An angel of God appears to Paul and tells him the ship will be destroyed, but all the men will live. Paul shared what the angel said with the men and added that he believed it would turn out that way. The ship runs aground, and all the men survive. If Paul had been saying, *"I don't believe the Word of God spoken by the angel and I believe we are all going to die,"* they would have had a different outcome. The other men already had no hope. Praise the Lord, the Word of God came, and Paul believed that WORD and spoke that WORD and the outcome was just as Paul had been told and just as Paul had spoken. Paul had to agree with the Word of God. Paul, speaking the Word of God, protected all of them and kept them safe. Paul could have opened wide his mouth and spoke the wrong things and negated the WORD about their protection. Speaking the Word of God can keep you safe and aren't you thrilled to know that your believing and speaking God's Word can keep others safe also.

Words Can Activate the Curse

WE READ IN SPEAKING TRUTH #11 HOW WORDS are associated with the blessing. This Speaking Truth is about how words are associated with the curse. In Numbers Chapter 22 the children of Israel were camped on the side of the River Jordan. Balak, king of Moab, was afraid of them because of their population and what they had done to the Amorites. Balak wants a man named Balaam to come and curse the children of Israel, so that he will be able to over-power them and drive them out of the land.[68] The word "curse" in Numbers 22:11 means "to utter the curse."[69] Balaam was to speak something to curse the children of Israel. This curse was to be activated by speaking words.

It was explained in the Introduction that words are things. Balak wants Balaam to speak words of the curse on the chil-dren of Israel. In wanting to cause harm to the children of Israel, Balak did not ask for Balaam to do things like poison them, send an army against them, set their camps on fire, or do anything physically to them. He simply wanted Balaam to cause the curse to manifest by speaking words. Why was just speaking words against Israel ok with Balak? It was okay because he and Balaam both knew that words are things. They both knew that words have power. They knew that words of the curse would produce outcomes (things) of the curse.

In Numbers 22:6 Balak made the remark that whom Balaam blessed was blessed, and whom Balaam cursed was cursed. It is worth noting that Balak had 100% confidence in Balaam's ability to speak words and it result in things of the blessing or things of the curse. Balak takes Balaam up where he could see the children of Israel below. While there, Balaam went to seek the Lord and was told what to pronounce concerning the children of Israel. Balaam spoke the Word from the Lord, and when he stopped speaking Balak said the following to him in Numbers 23:11.

> ¹¹And Balak said unto Balaam, What hast
> thou done unto me? I took thee to curse
> mine enemies, and, behold, thou hast blessed
> them altogether.
> Numbers 23:11, JKV

Balak comments that Balaam had blessed Israel. The only thing Balaam had done was speak. Balak considered the words that Balaam had just spoken as Balaam blessing the children of Israel. Speaking can activate the blessing or the curse.

Let's do as directed in Psalm 107:2 and speak as the redeemed. The redeemed should be saying something. Christ has redeemed us from the curse of the law and given us access to the blessing; therefore, the redeemed should be speaking words of the blessing. If you are believing and speaking words of the curse, it is an indication that things of the curse are in your heart more than things of the blessing. You've heard things of the curse more than you've heard the Word of God on the blessing and being redeemed. Change what you are believing and speaking by spending time hearing and hearing and hearing the Word of God, so that it gets in your heart in abundance and you begin to believe and speak words of the blessing and not the curse.

Your Words are Used to Make Your Confessions of Faith

HEBREWS CHAPTERS 2 AND 3 MAKES US AWARE that Jesus is the faithful high priest of our confession about who He is and what He has done. We can have complete confidence in confessing the Word of God and what Jesus has done for us. This is also why there is a section in the book on the Word of God. Hebrews 4:14 teaches that we are to hold fast our confession. The word confession is from a Greek compound word that means to speak the same as and to agree.[70] So, our confession would be us speaking the same as God's Word and in agreement with God's Word. The word "confession" is sometimes translated profession.[71] A profession is something that one does. Think about when someone is asked, "What is your profession?" They are being asked what it is that they do. We are to have a profession of confessing the Word of God. The confession we have to be making for Jesus to be high priest over is what the Word of God says. Jesus does not act apart from the Word of God.

The word confession is also related to the Greek word "lego," which can mean to speak a conclusion.[72] You know God speaks the end from the beginning.[73] We want the confessions that we speak to lead to the conclusions that God desires for our lives. For this to happen, we have to be confessing the Word of God. Romans 10:10 says confession is made unto salvation. Confession leads to something. What is confession? It is speaking. It is words, and words have outcomes. What did confession lead to for the woman who had the blood condition for 12 years? The Bible says she kept saying to herself what God's Word said about healing. She was not continually speaking that she had a blood condition. She was not continually saying that the physicians could not help her. These things were all facts, but instead of focusing on them and speaking them, she kept speaking about healing. She held fast to confessing words of healing and she saw healing in her life.

There are some in the Church who speak what we call confessions. We speak scriptures from the Word of God daily, weekly, and some may speak very specific ones several times a day when they are standing in faith for something specific. I believe having confessions as a part of your Christian life can accomplish several things, some of which are listed below.

1. Confession of the Word of God helps to get and keep the Word of God in your heart in abundance.

2. Confession of the Word of God is a way to do Joshua 1:8 in your life (it keeps the Word of God from departing from your mouth).

3. Confession of the Word of God builds your faith. Faith comes by hearing and hearing by the Word of God (even with you speaking it).

4. Confession of the Word of God gives your angels something to act on.

5. The Word of God is a seed and seeds need watering. According to Ephesians 5:26 there is a watering by the Word of God. Confession of the Word of God is how you keep that seed planted and watered until the harvest.

6. Confession of the Word of God contributes to you being transformed and it helps to keep your mind renewed.

Your Words Can Prevent You from Experiencing the Promises of God

In Mark chapter 6 Jesus went to minister in his hometown. He had preached and taught in many places by this time and had many miracles in His ministry. While there, Jesus went to the synagogue on the Sabbath and began to teach. Mark 6:2-4 describes what happened.

> ²And when the sabbath day was come, he began to teach in the synagogue: and many hearing him were astonished, saying, From whence hath this man these things? and what wisdom is this which is given unto him, that even such mighty works are wrought by his hands?
> ³Is not this the carpenter, the son of Mary, the brother of James, and Joses, and of Juda, and Simon? and are not his sisters here with us? And they were offended at him.

⁴But Jesus, said unto them, A prophet is not without honour, but in his own country, and among his own kin, and in his own house.
Mark 6:2-4, KJV

Many of the people who heard Jesus teaching in the synagogue were astonished at His teaching, and spoke negative things about Him. There were many in Jesus' hometown who did not receive Him as Messiah, or even as a prophet. We know what was in their hearts towards Jesus from what they spoke. As a result of the people doing this, Mark 6:5 records something that is eye opening. It points out that Jesus could not perform any miracles while in His hometown, and that He could only lay hands on a few sick people and heal them. What's the opposite of many? It is few. If many were saying things against Jesus, that means only a few people were not. It is therefore no coincidence that nothing happened for many and that only a few sick people were healed.

In many places where Jesus ministered the scriptures record that he healed many and multitudes. Do you think if the many had said, *"We've heard of the miracles performed by your hands and know you are a prophet of God"* that many would have been healed and miracles done? The people present knew that Jesus had performed miracles, because they said so in Mark 6:2, yet still rejected His ministry. This is a good place to highlight the boundaries of the hearts of the many who were speaking against Jesus' ministry. Their words did not go beyond Jesus being the carpenter, the son of Mary, and the brother of his siblings and their words kept them from experiencing the promise of God to heal and deliver His people.

For this Speaking Truth, we will read again about Zacharias, the Priest in Luke Chapter 1. You should remember from Speaking Truth #12 that the angel Gabriel appeared to him and told him that his prayer had been heard and that he and his wife would have a son. Zacharias (who was very old, and whose wife was very old and barren) wanted Gabriel to give him a sign that they would have the baby. Gabriel's response to Zacharias' request for a sign was that Zacharias would be unable to speak until the child was born, because he did not believe.[74] To keep Zacharias from speaking against the will of God and preventing it from coming to pass, Zacharias was unable to speak until after *John the Baptist* was born.

Zacharias had been praying to have a child. Gabriel comes and tells him what God said and Zacharias speaks words of unbelief. You can know faith by what one says, and you can know unbelief by what one says. Because of God's purpose for the life of *John the Baptist*, timing was of the essence. *John the Baptist* had to be the fore runner to Jesus. So, Zacharias did not need to be in unbelief about this and speaking against the Word of God. Once Zacharias became mute, he had his sign. The angel can't perform if you keep speaking against the Word of God. Once *John the Baptist* was born, Zacharias was able to speak again, when he could not speak against the Word of God about the birth of the child.

Zacharias had the story of the life of the patriarch Abraham to know how this works. And Praise God, we have the written Word of the Living God to know how this works also. Regardless of what it looks like, don't speak against the Word of God. Yes, Zacharias and his wife were old. Yes, Zacharias' wife was barren. In spite of all of this, what Zacharias needed to say about he and his wife's life was what God said. This is what Abraham did. Abraham started saying that he was the father of a multitude when he was old and when Sarah was old and barren. It would have been good if Zacharias had said, "*Glory to God we are having a baby*" or, "*I'm old, my wife is old, my wife is barren but God said we are having a son and we're having a son.*"

In II Kings Chapters 6 and 7 there was a severe famine. The prophet Elisha relayed the Word from the Lord to the king that there would be food at Samaria on the next day. The king's officer did not believe the Word of the Lord, and spoke against it. Elisha told the officer that there would definitely be food and that the officer would see it but not partake of any.

Four lepers went to the camp of the Syrian army and discovered that the men were gone. The Lord caused noise that made the Syrian army think another army was approaching. This resulted in the Syrian army fleeing and leaving everything behind. The lepers ate, gathered items from the camp, and decided to go and notify the king about what was available. The king sent men to ensure it was not an ambush. The men informed the king that everything was as the lepers reported. The king appointed his officer to oversee distribution of the food. However, the people rushed and trampled him. What the Word of the Lord announced was available, but the officer spoke against it and did not experience it in his life. We experience the promises of God through believing and speaking the right words. Our words can prevent us from experiencing what God has made available for us.

Section Three has a Speaking Truth from the Book of Job. Job's words prevented him from experiencing the goodness of God in his life for a period of time. This last Speaking Truth in Section Two is a good segue into reading about what happened with Job in Section Three.

Speaking Truth
From the Book of Job

A PERSON'S WORDS CAN CAUSE THEM TROUBLE and harm. Proverbs 21:23 declares that "Whoso keepeth his mouth and his tongue keepeth his soul from troubles."[75] Trouble is plural in this scripture, it is troubles. The reason it is plural is because until the person begins to guard what comes out of his/her mouth they prolong the potential for experiencing more problems and trouble in their life as a result of their believing and speaking. Proverbs 13:3 warns about the mouth and destruction. It says, "He that keepeth his mouth keepeth his life: but he that openeth wide his lips shall have destruction."[76] A man's lips can either preserve his life or cause destruction. There is however, good news in Proverbs 13:2 which tells us that a man can enjoy good by the words of his mouth. Your words can cause you to enjoy good (this sounds like Psalms 34:12-13). As you read Speaking Truth 20 you will recognize these scriptures in Job's life.

Ephesians 4:27 commands us to not give the devil a spot or opportunity in our lives. We are not to give the devil place, because he only comes to steal, kill, and destroy. I Peter 5:8 charges us to be sober and vigilant because the devil goes about seeking whom he may devour. There are things that can give the devil place in one's life. Words are one of those things. The word "sober" used here is defined as "discreet" and "circumspect."[77] One way to be discreet is to be careful in one's speech or actions. To assist us with being sober we are to be guarded in our speech. We read scriptures about guarding our mouths in Section Two and I Pet 5:8 gives an indication that we should be guarded in our speech, because of the devil. What sometimes happens when people are intoxicated (not sober)? Some of them absolutely do not guard their speech. Some talk all the more, allowing anything to come out of their mouths. But one doesn't have to be intoxicated to not be sober in their speech. They can simply be someone who just allows anything to come out of their mouth.

I Peter 5:8 also exposes something else for us, the devil can't just devour whomever he wants. He goes about looking for whom he *may* devour. If he could just devour any and all humans, he would have destroyed all mankind a long time ago. The one who has the potential to not be devoured is the one who is sober and vigilant. One way to be sober is by guarding your speech. Things you say can give the devil access to your life to cause you problems, troubles, adversity, calamity, suffering, thief, death, and destruction.

Many people possibly avoid the Book of Job because of the adversity experienced by Job. Satan showed up in Job's life and caused theft, death, and destruction. There is a lot in the Book of Job about speaking. Job speaks about his words, Job has three friends who speak about Job's words, Satan says Job will speak a certain way, a young man named Elihu speaks about Job's words, and the Lord speaks about Job's words. I believe all of this is a good indication that God wants us to learn something about words in the Book of Job. This Section of the Book will emphasize how Job's words contributed to what he saw (experienced in his life).

Words Can Give Place
to the Devil

THIS IS THE ONLY SPEAKING TRUTH FOR SECTION Three. The Book of Job starts by describing some things about Job and acquainting us with his life. He had children, servants, land, livestock, lived in the land of Uz, and was extremely rich. Job feared God, shunned evil, was upright, and had integrity. Satan appeared twice when the sons of God came to present themselves before the Lord. Why was Satan coming? I believe he was coming to be an accuser against Job (he's identified as an accuser in Revelation 12:10). The Lord asked Satan where he came from and Satan replied, "From going to and fro in the earth, and from walking up and down in it."[78] This response resembles I Peter 5:8. The Lord then asked Satan if he had set his heart against Job. Satan suggested that the Lord harm Job, so that it leads to Job cursing the Lord. Actually, Satan wants all mankind to believe that the Lord is harming them, thus resulting in some of them hating God, cursing God, and wanting nothing to do with God.

Although, Satan suggested that the Lord afflict Job, you'll notice the Lord did not. I want to mention something about the Lord denoting in Job 2:3 that Satan had incited Him to destroy Job without cause. The phrase, "without cause" can be translated useless, in vain, or for naught.[79] Satan inciting the Lord to harm Job was not useless, in vain, and for naught, because Job had done nothing wrong. It was useless, in vain, and for naught because the Lord is not the thief, the killer, or the destroyer. John 10:10 details what Jesus does and what Satan does. Jesus gives life and life more abundantly, while Satan steals, kills, and destroys. We don't read anywhere in the Gospels where Jesus harmed people, stole from people, killed people, or destroyed things in people's lives. If it steals, kills, or destroys, it is of Satan.

Satan describes a hedge that the Lord had put around Job, his household, and around everything Job had. The Lord makes it known that there are things in Job's life that are already in Satan's hand, with the exception of Job's life.[80] This hedge that Satan talked about was now broken for certain areas of Job's life. According to Ecclesiastes 10:8 a serpent will strike or oppress one who breaks a hedge and Satan is referred to as a serpent in Revelation 12:9. Part of the hedge for areas of Job's life was broken and Satan (the serpent) now had an opportunity to come through and bring theft, death, and destruction. How did the hedge get broken for these areas of Job's life and get in Satan's hand? Job's words are one way the hedge got broken.

We learned in Job 1:10 about this hedge God had put in place for Job, but Job did not believe and speak that the hedge was for his good. Job believes the hedge is something that God puts in place to make it impossible for a person to escape affliction and continual harm.

> [20]Wherefore is light given to him that is in
> misery, and life unto the bitter in soul;
> [21]Which long for death, but it cometh not;
> and dig for it more than for hid treasures;
> [22]Which rejoice exceedingly, and are glad,
> when they can find the grave?
> [23]Why is light given to a man whose way is
> hid, and whom God hath hedged in?
> Job 3:20-23, KJV

There is more evidence of Job believing this in Job 19:6-8. This belief and speaking are two of the things that caused the hedge to be broken for certain areas of Job's life. How did the Lord put the hedge in place for Job? The same way we learned in Speaking Truth #1 about how the Lord does everything. The Lord put the hedge in place for Job with His Words. How was the hedge broken for certain areas of Job's life? The hedge was broken the same way the hedge was put in place. The hedge was put in place with words and the hedge was broken with words. Job's words caused the hedge that the Lord put in place for him to be broken in certain areas and it gave place to Satan.

Satan said that the Lord put the hedge in place, and because of it there were very good things in Job's life. The Lord has done many good things for us that we have to receive. We receive by believing in our hearts and speaking with our mouths. What's in our hearts will come out of our mouths. This is similar to salvation. God has made salvation available to every person, through Jesus. We have to receive this salvation by believing it in our hearts and confessing it with our mouths. This is how we receive all things from God's Word, by believing in our hearts and speaking it with our mouths. Satan knew the results of the hedge being there (he spoke it in Job 1:10). Job needed to believe and speak the right things about the hedge and other areas of his life to keep the blessing of the hedge in place.

Let's review some things that Job believed and spoke concerning his children from Job Chapter 1. Job's sons and daughters had feasts, and afterwards Job would sanctify them and offer burnt offerings for them. Job tells us in Job 1:5 why he offered the burnt offerings. He said he offered them because, "It may be that my sons have sinned, and cursed God in their hearts."[81] It also says in Job 1:5 that Job did something all the time. From reading this scripture, I believe Job did these things all time:

1) Sanctified his children and offer burnt offer-ings for them
2) He said something all the time.

What was it that Job said all the time? Job said this all the time, "Maybe my sons have sinned and cursed God in their hearts."

Job was not just casually saying this. Job believed (was convinced) that his children had sinned. How do we know this? We know this because of two things stated in Job 1:5:

1) Job said it all the time and what is in the heart in abundance comes out of the mouth all the time
2) Job acted on it all the time (Job actually offered burnt offerings because his children sinning was that real to him).

Burnt offerings were offered, because sin had occurred (when someone had actually sinned). They were not required just in case one may sin. Since Job was actually offering the burnt offerings, it was because Job was convinced (fully persuaded) in his heart that his children had sinned and he spoke it and acted on it. Regardless of whether Job saw them sin or not, their sinning was so real to him that he actually offered burnt offerings for them. This was total believeth in things not seen.

If you are thinking that this language that I'm using that Job was convinced and fully persuaded of things not seen sounds like faith, you are correct. It does sound like faith, but instead of faith, it is fear. This type fear is being convinced of and expecting for something bad or unpleasant to certainly happen. This does sound like faith language, because there is a component of faith that involves expecting and being convinced of what you don't see yet. Job was in fear about his children sinning and cursing God in their hearts. He believed this, spoke it, expected it, acted on it, and it caused the hedge to be broken in this area of his life.

Job also had this belief and spoke it, "Naked (without possessions) came I [into this world] from my mother's womb, and naked (without possessions) shall I depart."[82] Job probably did not just start believing this way. His believing and speaking this way gave Satan access to steal and destroy his possessions. In Job 1:14-17, Job lost some things that he had obtained since coming into the world. Because the hedge was broken in certain areas, these were some of the things Satan caused to happen to Job:

1) He had servants killed (Job 1:16)
2) He had livestock destroyed (Job 1:16)
3) People came and took away his livestock (Job 1:14; Job 1:17).

Job's words caused the hedge to be broken in these areas. Let's learn from this and be certain to believe, and speak in agreement with the Word of God. Instead of saying I came into the world with nothing and will depart with nothing, let's say, "*I will leave an inheritance to my children and grandchildren.*"

People often quote Job 1:21. There is a popular saying about things not being pulled behind a hearse that is possibly rooted in Job 1:21. People don't take their earthly belongings with them when they die, but be guarded in forming a certain belief and speaking this way. Job believed this saying, spoke it, and lost what he had while he was still living. He did not lose the things in Job 1:14-17 after he died. Job lost them while he was still living on the earth and could have still used them. Believing this way and speaking this way can prevent people from acquiring things and keeping them if they have them.

There are statements in the Bible that are things men believed and spoke, which are not Words that God spoke and that do not agree with Words God has spoken. You'll see more examples of this as we continue in the Book of Job.

Be on the alert for subtle ways in which one can be deceived into believing and speaking wrong things. There are voices in the world right now that say it is not a good thing to leave an inheritance to your children, but agree with and speak the Word of God. He not only wants you to leave an inheritance to your children, He wants you to leave an inheritance to your grandchildren too. Don't get in agreement with and speak things that are contrary to the Word of God. Desire and speak for the Lord to prosper you, so that you have plenty to give to every good work and to leave an inheritance to your children and grandchildren.

I believe Job's life was not in Satan's hand like the other areas because the hedge was not broken when it came to his life. I noticed two distinct things it seems Job had **not** been believing in his heart and speaking harmful things, unpleasant things, things not desired, or things of the curse about:

1) His wife
2) His life.

There are scriptures where Job had spoken good about both of these areas of his life and the hedge was not broken for these areas. When it came to Job's wife, he was not believing in his heart, and speaking things of the curse. Job 31:1 reveals something Job believed and spoke about his marriage. It was that he had made a covenant with his eyes and would not look on or consider other women. Also, notice that Job was not speaking about and offering burnt offerings for his wife the way he had done for his children.

When it came to Job's life, we get an idea from Job 29:18 of why the hedge was not broken and why Satan could not kill Job. This scripture makes us aware of what was in Job's heart, and what he had spoken about his life and dying. It was believing and speaking to live long and die in his dwelling. Job was not believing in his heart and speaking the wrong things when it came to the length of his life. His words for a long life were aligned with Psalm 91:16 (that we live a long and satisfied life). He missed the satisfied part, but his believing got adjusted about it later.

Chapter 29 provides more information about Job's life. He did not fear dying young or from calamity. Job had not given Satan access to destroy his life. There are scriptures where he spoke of wanting to die, but Job was not consistent in speaking this way. In Chapter 29 Job recalls how his life was and he desired to live that way again. You can read in Job 42:17 that Job died after living a long life, just as he had believed in his heart and spoken. The Young's Literal Translation actually has the word 'satisfied' in this verse. Job lived a long and satisfied life.

In response to the adversity that Job experienced in Chapter 1, Job makes the statement, "The LORD gave, and the LORD hath taken away."[83] What's recorded next in Job 1:22 is significant. It says that Job neither sinned nor charged God with wrongdoing. Job did not do as Satan had predicted. He did not curse God. Job was wrong in believing and saying that the Lord gives and takes away because the Lord does not take away. The Lord indeed gave to Job, but he did not take anything away from Job. Man may lose things and Satan may steal and destroy things, but the Lord does not take things away from us. The Lord is a giver. What Job said about God was wrong, but at this point Job did not charge God with a wrong. Here Job was not believing and speaking that God was unjust and mistreating him. It's interesting that the word "charge" is used in Job 1:22. How is someone charged with wrongdoing or accused of wrongdoing in the judicial world? They are charged by speaking, the charges are pronounced (they are spoken).

Job 2:10 is another significant scripture about Job's words. Job made an incorrect statement again about the adversity he was experiencing when he said to his wife that they should accept both good and evil from God. Job is speaking something wrong because God does not cause evil. Also, it's very, very clear from Job 1:12 and Job 2:7 that the evil is coming from Satan. The last sentence in Job 2:10 mentions again that Job was not sinning with his lips. The WORD pointing this out is important. Indicating that Job was not sinning with his lips was referring to what Job had just said in reaction to what was happening to him. Job was saying something wrong, but not accusing God of wrongdoing or cursing God. There are scriptures in the Bible that indicate that we can sin with our lips (Psalm 17:3, Psalm 39:1 and Psalm 59:12 are a few). Job 2:10 is the last time the Book of Job indicates that Job was not sinning with his lips. Once Chapter 4 starts, people even begin to speak to Job about problems with his words.

In Chapter 1, Job experienced the death of his children, servants and livestock and he had things stolen and destroyed. Job's health is attacked in Chapter 2. Job also talked about losing his stature and profession. Job describes something else that caused theft, death, and destruction in areas of his life with his statement in Job 3:25 that what he feared came upon him and what he dreaded happened to him. Some may tend to think of fear as a feeling one can get while watching a scary movie. But this type fear in the Book of Job is believing, speaking, and expecting that harmful things, unpleasant things, things not desired, or things of the curse are coming to pass in one's life. It is being convinced and fully persuaded of this. Faith is believing in the heart, speaking, and expecting the promises and blessing of the Word of God to come to pass in one's life. Job's statement in Job 3:25 about what he feared and what he dreaded happening to him reveals to us that he had believed these things in his heart, had spoken them with his mouth, and had expected for them to happen.

What Job feared and dreaded happened to him. We've discussed the fear, now what about the dread? In Job 13:11, Job speaks about the *dread of God* coming upon people. Dread is great fear, especially in the face of impending evil.[84] Job tells his friends when God examines people that this *dread of God* (an impending evil from God) will happen to them. Job speaking about this *dread of God* happening to him indicates that he had believed in his heart, spoken, and expected that God would cause evil and harm in his life. He had an expectation for it. This is why he said what he did about his children and performed those burnt offerings. He was persuaded that the *dread of* God would happen. Job's belief in this *dread of God* was so embedded in his heart that only the Lord Himself could convince Job that Job was wrong in believing and speaking this way.

Job has three friends that came to visit him (Eliphaz, Bildad, and Zophar). There is a pattern in the Book of Job where Job's friends speak, and Job responds. These three friends, and a young man named Elihu, say something directly to Job about Job's words at least 14 times (see Appendix A).

Eliphaz is the first to speak and points out to Job that there is a difference in the wicked and the righteous. Job believed and spoke that there was not. To believe and speak that there is no difference in the wicked and the righteous is wrong believing and speaking. There are many scriptures in the Psalms and Book of Proverbs that bear witness that there is a difference in the righteous and the wicked. Think about this, if there is no distinction for the righteous, then on the Day of Judgment, the righteous will be cast into hell, along with Satan and the wicked. No, through the Blood and redemptive works of Jesus Christ, God has given the righteous eternal life and not eternal damnation with Satan in hell. This type believing and speaking that Job did in Job 9:22 is indicting God with wrong. Eliphaz tells Job that Job's own words are condemning him, and that Job's lips are testifying against him.[85]

Job's friend Bildad begins to address Job in Chapter 8. Bildad starts by asking Job, "How long wilt thou speak these things? and how long shall the words of thy mouth be like a strong wind?"[86] This scripture reminds me of the word "windbag." Bildad asks Job again, in Job 18:2, when is he going to stop talking. The first time Job's third friend, Zophar, begins to speak is in Chapter 11. How does Zophar start? Zophar begins by saying something to Job about Job's words. He paints a picture for us of Job having a multitude of words and being full of talk.[87] Are you noticing something? People are continuing to say something to Job about his words. Eliphaz pleads with Job to lay up God's Words in his heart and to return to the Almighty. Why does Job need to lay up God's Word in his heart? Job needs to do this so that God's Word is what comes out of his mouth and is what he will see in his life. The last time one of Job's three friends attempted to help him was in Chapter 25.

There are many instances where Job charged God with wrongdoing or with harming him (some are listed in Appendix B). He believed that the terrors of God were arranged against him. He accused God of bruising him and wounding him without cause. Job is incriminating God with wrongdoing, by declaring first that God harms people and second that God does so for no reason. Both beliefs are not true. Job wants to know what he has done to God to cause God to make him his target. He asserts that God would not pardon his transgression and take away his iniquity. God sent Jesus to forgive us of our transgressions, but we have to repent and ask for this forgiveness. Scripture has in I John 1:9, "If we confess our sins, he is faithful and just to forgive us our sins, and to cleanse us from all unrighteousness."[88]

Job conveyed in Job 14:19 that God destroys man's hope. However, Romans 15:13 identifies God as the God of hope. Job's believing and speaking that God destroys man's hope also violates Jeremiah 17:7, which teaches that the man who hopes in the Lord is blessed. We are not to believe that the Lord destroys man's hope, but rather that the man who hopes in the Lord is blessed. Job is bold in proclaiming that the beasts, the birds, the earth, and the fish can all verify that the hand of the Lord has caused his adversity.[89] The hand of the Lord was not, rather it was Satan attacking Job. When

Satan said for the Lord to put His hand against Job, the Lord did not.

Job has made crucial statements, in which he blamed God for what was happening to him, and plainly declares in Job 19:6 that God had wronged him. Job's not quite finished with his multitude of words just yet. He starts a discourse in Chapter 26 that ends with Chapter 31. During this discourse some of the things that Job voiced was that God had taken away his justice, made his soul bitter, and spoiled his success. Job ends his discourse by expressing that he would have been deserving of what happened to him, if he had done certain things like allowing himself to be allured by a woman, mistreating his workers, the poor, the widow, or the hungry, being in pride, rejoicing in the ruin of his enemies, or obtained his land inappropriately (read Job Chapter 31 for the complete list). Job probably did not do any of these things, but one thing he did do was fail to guard his mouth.

Job has talked and talked, until he finally stops talking at the end of Chapter 31. In Chapter 32, a young man named Elihu starts his discourse. Elihu has heard conversations between Job and his three friends and noticed that Job's three friends had failed to help him. Elihu kept quiet, while the three older men spoke, but the Almighty gave him understanding and he appealed to them to listen to him. Elihu, just like Job's three friends, says things to Job about what Job had been saying. He recaps several things that Job believed and said about God that were not true. In Chapter 34, Elihu reminds Job that he had said that it does not benefit a person to delight in God. This statement contradicts Psalm 37:4, where we are encouraged to delight ourselves in the Lord and He will give us the desires of our heart. There is benefit for delighting in the Lord. For speaking this way, Elihu told Job that he was consuming scorn like water and behaving as those who are workers of iniquity. With the things Job had been saying about God, he was accusing God of being unjust and doing things that were evil. Elihu stressed to Job that God can't engage in wickedness or iniquity and that God would never pervert justice. Doing evil things and being unjust is impossible for God. I John 1:5 emphatically establishes, that "God is light, and in him is no darkness at all."[90] In Job 34:35-37, Elihu communicates about Job; that he is speaking without knowledge, that he is speaking without wisdom, that he is speaking as wicked men, that he has sin and rebellion, and that he is speaking against God. Time and time again Job uttered things about God that were not true. He was speaking against the truth of the Word of God.

Elihu provides a list of things about God that are true in Job 36:9-10:

1) God makes people to know their transgressions
2) God let's people know about their pride
3) God opens man's ears to instruction
4) God tells man to turn from iniquity.

The next verse (Job 36:11) tells us that God does these things so that the one who obeys and serve Him will live their days in prosperity and experience their years being pleasant. Elihu emphasized that God would have brought Job out of affliction, but Job became full of judgment. Job was actually judging the Lord. This resulted in a disruption in Job spending his days in prosperity and his years in pleasures. It prevented the Lord from delivering Job at that time, and bringing Job to a place where nothing was withheld from him, and where he experienced the best. You can't believe for God to deliver you, if at the same time you are believing and speaking that God is the one harming you.

The Book of Job outlines some of the things that befalls the wicked in Chapters 15 and 18, and for several months conditions in Job's life resembled that of the wicked. Job was correct when he identified that he was experiencing some of the same things as the wicked. Job was not correct about why it was happening and who was harming him. Elihu, setting forth in Job 36:17, that Job was filled with judgment is interesting. Job had been believing that judgment would happen to him and his children. He spoke about this judgment as the *dread of God*. Job's heart was full of what he referred to as the *dread of God*. His conviction about this led him to speak continually of it and offer burnt offerings for his children. Job's belief (conviction) about this *dread of God* is why he said what he did in Job 3:25, about what he feared and dreaded happening to him. His believing in his heart, speaking about these things of judgment, and expecting it to happen caused it to happen to him. What was in Job's heart in abundance (what his heart was full of) is what came out of his mouth and it determined what came forth in his life. We read about this in Speaking Truth #13.

Elihu finishes speaking in Chapter 37. Now for the Finale. The Lord begins to speak to Job in Chapter 38, and He starts by asking Job a question. Job had expressed in Chapters 10 and 13 that he would question or inquire of God. So, what does the Lord do? He corrects and instructs Job, by answering questions and asking Job questions. The first thing the Lord says to Job is, "Who is this that darkens counsel by words without knowledge?"[91] What's happening here is of herculean proportion. The first thing the Lord says to Job is something about **Job's words**. Job had remarked that he wanted the Lord to tell him where he had erred. Here it is. Here is the answer. It was Job's words. The Lord revealed to Job that he had erred in his speaking. Chapter 1 identified Job as being perfect and upright. Being perfect and upright does not mean that one does not sometimes do wrong, miss the mark, make mistakes, or sin. Job had erred in what he had been believing in his heart and speaking with his mouth, and it caused the adversity he was experiencing. Even when it came to the fear and the *dread of God*, Job believed those things in his heart, was convinced of them, spoke them, and was expecting them to happen. His words still played a role in it. Job's three friends and Elihu had all said things to him about what he had been saying and now the Lord is telling Job the same thing: Job, there is a problem with your words.

As you read Chapters 38 through the end of 41, notice how the Lord is correcting and instructing Job. The Lord is doing this by speaking to Job, not by harming and afflicting Job. He's correcting and instructing by teaching Job with His Word. The awesome, loving, and compassionate nature of the Lord is on display in His correction of Job. The Lord is teaching Job precious truths about creation and things of nature, while at the same time correcting Job (ten of these truths are listed in Appendix C). This is how the Lord corrects and instructs. He does it in love with His Word.

At the beginning of Chapter 40, the Lord says something to Job about finding fault with Him and asks Job to provide an answer. Job's response is, "Behold, I am vile; what shall I answer thee? I will lay mine hand upon my mouth."[92] Job acknowledges in Job 40:5 that he has spoken too much and indicates that he will say no more. After the Lord's correction of Job, Job leaves no doubt that he understands there has been a problem with what he has been saying. Job says in Job 42:3 that he had spoken things that he did not understand. While repenting, Job says to the Lord, "Therefore I retract [my words and hate myself] And I repent in dust and ashes."[93] This entire saga was connected to Job's words. Job was "Saying and Seeing."

The Lord spoke to Job in four chapters (38, 39, 40 and 41). As the Lord was speaking to Job, the Word of God was going forth and Job was hearing and hearing the Word of God and it got in his heart in abundance. Job recognized that his own words had been the problem after hearing and hearing as the Lord was speaking. Job repented and it changed the rest of his life for the better. We saw the good that happened when Job repented. When Job repented, he changed how he believed and spoke, and there was good in his life again.[94] Things of the blessing were on the other side of Job's repentance. God's goodness is connected to repentance.[95] It was the goodness of God that revealed to Job where he had erred and that lead to Job's repenting. The good life and things of the blessing were on the other side of Job changing his words to align with the Word of God. When Job retracted his words, he did not continue to speak the way he had been speaking.

Chapter 42 describes for us how the latter end of Job's life was more blessed than the former. Job actually experienced what Bildad had said in Job 8:7, about his latter end being greatly increased.[96] Job also experienced what Eliphaz had said to him in Job 5:17, Job 5:25, and Job 22:25. Eliphaz said in Job 5:17 that the man whom God corrects will be blessed. Reading Job 42:12 we see that the Lord blessed Job. Job received the correction of the Lord and experienced the blessing in his life again. Eliphaz went on to say in Job 5:25 that Job would know (realize by seeing and being acquainted with) children and many grandchildren if he received correction from God.[97] At this point, for Job to see and be acquainted with children, Job would have to have more children (remember Job's children were destroyed). This happened for Job in Job 42:13-16 where we read that Job had 10 more children and lived to see his children and grandchildren to four generations. Isn't Job 42:15 exciting? Job gave an inheritance to his sons and daughters. He was no longer going around making statements about, "*The Lord giving and taking away and leaving the world with nothing.*" Eliphaz had also said in Job 22:23-25 if Job returned to the Almighty that gold and silver would accompany it. Job repented and returned to the Almighty, and in Job 42:11 the gold and silver begin showing up. Hallelujah, it is okay to prosper with the Lord.

Job experienced things that Zophar had said to him. One of which was that Job's head would be lifted up, if he put away iniquity and kept wickedness out of his dwelling. This came to pass for Job in Job 42:9, when his face was lifted up. Do you recognize something when you read what happened to Job in Job 42:9, Job 42:11, Job 42:12, Job 42:13, and Job 42:16? The Word of God was being confirmed with signs following, the Word of God was not returning void, and God had watched over His Word to perform it in Job's life. What Elihu said in Job 36:9-10 also came to pass. The Lord made Job to know his transgressions, He opened Job's ears to instruction, and Job turned from iniquity. The result was Job obeying and serving God and living the rest of his days in prosperity and having his years be pleasant. We don't read about Job having that type calamity again. Job's life was long and satisfied.

It is very common to hear that God caused Job's problems to teach Job something or to teach Job patience. We read in Chapters 38 through 41 how the Lord corrected and taught Job by speaking His Word to Job, not by causing harm to Job. It is also very common to hear that God may not have caused Job's adversity, but God allowed Satan to harm Job. Job gave the devil place in his life, with his believing and speaking. We've seen two things in the Book of Job that gave the devil place in Job's life:

1) What Job was saying
2) Fear (believing, speaking, and expecting for harmful, evil or unpleasant things, things not desired, or things of the curse to happen in one's life).

Job disclosed to us about the fear in Job 3:25, and the Lord revealed to us about Job's words being a problem in Job 38:2.

The content for Speaking Truth #12 covered how your words can cause your angels to work on your behalf. In that Speaking Truth we gained the understanding that angels hear, listen to, and obey the voice of the Lord's Word. These angels are the ones who listen for one to speak the Lord's Word and they act. Satan (the devil) is a fallen angel, and he also listens for words.[98] He listens for words that are opposite the Word of God and words of the curse. He listens for these type words to obey, accomplish, perform, and bring forth. Job believed in his heart and spoke words that allowed Satan to bring them to pass in his life. Job's failure to guard his mouth resulted in him not being sober in his speaking and it gave the devil access to bring theft, death, and destruction. The Lord said something to Job's three friends about their words, and it did not take them months of calamity to change. As soon as the Lord told them that they had spoken things that were not right and for them to offer a burnt offering, they went into action. Some seize on how the Lord said something to Job's three friends about their words, but pay no attention to the Lord saying something to Job about Job's words also.

Job did a lot of talking. One of his friends even commented that Job had a multitude of words. Job said himself in Job 3:26 that he was not at ease (tranquil, prosperous, secure, safe, happy, or successful), he was not quiet, he had no rest, and trouble came.[99] This was because he was saying the wrong things. If you believe in your heart and keep speaking the wrong things, it can lead to no ease, no prosperity, no safety, no rest, and trouble. Job divulged in Job 9:20 that, although he was righteous, his own mouth condemned him and that his mouth proved perversion. Proverbs 4:24 commands that we put perverse lips far away from us. Job was speaking things that were contrary to the Word of God. What was happening to Job was indeed that his own mouth was condemning him and causing him much adversity. Psalms 34:12-13 high-lighted for us that the person who speaks things that are false (not the truth) or things that are treacherous (not of faith) will not be pleased with life and see many good days. Job experienced a period where he was not pleased with life and did not see many good days because of his words.

In Job 13:13, Job demanded that his friends be silent and let him speak, and let come on him what may. Job was not heeding their words about what he was saying. Job was not guarding what words came out of his mouth. He was speaking things that were not the truth of the Word of God. He was speaking things of the curse and what may (things of the curse) was coming on him. Job was speaking, and speaking, and speaking and letting come on him what may. You can control what comes on you and what happens in your life by guarding what words come out of your mouth.

After Job heard, and heard, and heard the Word of God as the Lord was correcting him, Job repented and changed his speaking. How do we know Job changed his speaking? Because of the following:

1) What comes forth in one's life is from believing and speaking
2) You can have what you say that you believe
3) The one who is pleased with life and sees many good days is the one who speaks the right way.

Job saw many good days and was pleased with life again after he repented and retracted his words. Job had been believing and speaking many things that were opposite the

Word of God and his life reflected it. As we read about what came forth in Job's life, in Job 42:12-16, it resembles the promises and the blessing in the Word of God. What was now in Job's heart in abundance was coming out of his mouth and coming forth in his life.

The Book of Job demonstrates the importance of our words, the role they play in our lives and why we should ensure that we are speaking the Word of God. Job was not sober (guarded in his speech) and it gave the devil place in his life to steal, kill, and destroy. We are to be vigilant about guarding our words. Speaking the Word of God allows us to be guarded in our speech. Speaking the Word of God allows us to speak things that are Truth and things that are of Faith. When our words are not the right words, let's be like Job and retract them and begin to say what God's Word says so that we see what God desires for our lives.

Closing Words

TWENTY SPEAKING TRUTHS PROVIDED EXAM-
ples about the importance of speaking God's Word. Revelation
1:4-6 reveals that Jesus Christ has made Christians kings and
priests to His God and Father. Kings understood the significance of their words and that their words had power. As
kings and priests unto God the Father, let's speak the Word
of God, so that God can confirm it and show forth Jesus and
His goodness to the world that God so loves.

We also want to be people speaking the Word of God
because of situations and things in the world that are not
good (darkness). The Bible speaks of more of this in the end
times. Light, however, can overcome darkness and God's
Word brings light. Psalms 119:130 says the entrance of God's
Word gives light. This is what we saw happen in Genesis
1:2-3. It was the Word of God being spoken that overcame
that darkness. It was the speaking of the Word of God that
paved the way for light to come. I noticed another example
of this in Isaiah Chapters 59 and 60. In Isaiah 60:1-3 we see
light come where there is darkness. If you read Isaiah 59:21
(the last verse before Isaiah 60), it's about speaking the Word
of God. It's about keeping the Word of God coming out of
the mouth. Right before the light appears in Isaiah 60:1-2

during darkness, in Isaiah 59:21 the Word of God was to be spoken and spoken and spoken and the Lord said to speak it forevermore. As we look at the ministry of Jesus we notice how often He did things by speaking. God needs Believers not only praying in this earth but also declaring His Word.

Psalms 34:12-13 gave us insight into what the person does who wants to be pleased with life and see many good days. That person has to speak a certain way. We have to keep from speaking the wrong things, because *Saying is connected to Seeing*. The best way to keep from speaking the wrong thing is to speak the Word of God and in agreement with the Word of God. Let's say what God SAYs so that we SEE (have and experience) what God desires in the Church and for our lives.

Salvation Prayer

CHRIST HAS REDEEMED US FROM THE CURSE OF the law. Jesus has made available a wonderful Redemptive Life for us. The first step to living this Redemptive Life is to receive Jesus as your Lord and Savior, by praying this prayer.

Father God, I believe your Word that you sent Jesus and that He died on the cross and paid for my sins. Father God, I believe that you raised Jesus from the dead and that He is alive forevermore. I repent and I believe that the precious blood of Jesus washes away all of my sins. Jesus I accept what you did for me and I ask you to come into my heart and save me, and to make me a new creation in you. Fill me with your Holy Spirit. I believe that I am now a born again child of God. I pray this in Jesus Name. *Amen*

You are now born again and will notice a change in your heart. There is joy in heaven over you coming into the Kingdom of God (Luke 15:7). Find a good Church to begin growing in the things of God. If you prayed this prayer please let us know by sending an email to SayingandSeeing@att.net.

APPENDICES

Appendix A

Scriptures of Job's 3 Friends and Elihu Saying Something About Job's Words

Job 8:1-2

Job 18:1-2

Job 11:1-2

Job 11:3

Job 15:1-3

Job 15:5

Job 15:6

Job 15:12-13

Job 33:8-12

Job 34:5-9

Job 34:17-18

Job 34:35-37

Job 35:1-3

Job 35:16

Appendix B

Scripture References for Job Speaking the Wrong Things

Job Referring to God as the One Causing His Afflictions	Job Charging God with Wrong/ Speaking Untruths About God
Job 2:10	Job 1:21
Job 6:4	Job 7:21
Job 6:9	Job 9:22
Job 7:20	Job 9:23
Job 9:13-18	Job 10:1-3
Job 10:2	Job 14:19
Job 10:8	Job 19:6
Job 10:14-20	Job 19:8
Job 19:21-22	Job 19:11
Job 30:20-21	Job 27:2
	Job 34:9

Appendix C

Things About Nature and Creation the Lord Shared with Job

1. The seas have doors (Job 38:8).
2. The waves of the sea were commanded how far they could go (Job 38:10-11).
3. Dawn has a place (Job 38:12).
4. Light and Darkness both have homes (Job 38:19-20).
5. There is a treasury of snow and hail (Job 38:22-23).
6. The young of the raven cry to God for food (Job 38:41).
7. The ostrich leaves her eggs on the ground but this also puts them in danger (Job 39:14-15).
8. Horses are frightened by locusts, but not of going into a battle (Job 39:19-22).
9. Information about the first animal in creation. The animal eats grass like an ox; has strength in his hips; has powerful stomach muscles; has a tail; has sinews in his thighs that are tightly knit; has bones like bronze; has ribs like bars of iron; lies under trees in a covert of reeds and marsh; seeks shade from these trees; can have water rage and it not be disturbed by it; and can have the river gush into its mouth and into its

eyes (Job 40:15-24). This animal has features of the hippopotamus.

10. Information about a creature that if man tries to pet it, man will never forget the battle (Job 41:1-8).

ENDNOTES

1   Psalm 107:2, NKV
2   OT:562 and OT:1697, Strong's Exhaustive Concordance of the Bible 1st ed. Copyright © 1988, by Hendrickson Publishers.
3   OT:7451, Strong's Exhaustive Concordance of the Bible 1st ed. Copyright © 1988, by Hendrickson Publishers; New American Standard Exhaustive Concordance of the Bible with Hebrew-Aramaic and Greek Dictionaries. Copyright © 1981, 1998 by The Lockman Foundation.
4   OT:4820, Strong's Exhaustive Concordance of the Bible 1st ed. Copyright © 1988, by Hendrickson Publishers.
5   "treachery." *Merriam-Webster.com. Dictionary*, Merriam-Webster, https://www.merriam-webster.com/dictionary/treachery. Accessed 11 November 2019.
6   John 17:17
7   Genesis 1:3, YLT
8   Genesis 1:26, KJV
9   Genesis 22:17
10 Matthew 9:21, NASB
11 Luke 1:38, KJV
12 Luke 5:5, KJV
13 OT:85, Strong's Exhaustive Concordance of the Bible 1st ed. Copyright © 1988, by Hendrickson Publishers.
14 OT:8282, Strong's Exhaustive Concordance of the Bible 1st ed. Copyright © 1988, by Hendrickson Publishers.
15 Genesis 21:1-3
16 Hebrews 11:7, NASB
17 Luke 1:45, KJV
18 Genesis 1:11-12
19 Ephesians 5:26
20 Mark 4:26
21 OT:226, Strong's Exhaustive Concordance of the Bible 1st ed. Copyright © 1988, by Hendrickson Publishers; NT:4592, Strong's Exhaustive Concordance of the Bible 1st ed. Copyright © 1988, by Hendrickson Publishers; New American Standard Exhaustive Concordance of the Bible with Hebrew-Aramaic and Greek Dictionaries. Copyright © 1981, 1998 by The Lockman Foundation.

22 OT:4832, Strong's Exhaustive Concordance of the Bible 1st ed. Copyright © 1988, by Hendrickson Publishers.

23 Matthew 12:34, KJV

24 Psalm 107:20, KJV

25 Matthew 8:8

26 NT:436, Strong's Exhaustive Concordance of the Bible 1st ed. Copyright © 1988, by Hendrickson Publishers.

27 Ephesians 6:17, KJV

28 Matthew 4:4, KJV

29 Genesis 3:4

30 Matthew 4:7, KJV

31 2 Samuel 7:13; Obadiah 21; Isaiah 9:-7; Micah 4:7; Luke 1:30-33

32 Matthew 12:36, KJV

33 Proverbs 18:21, NASB

34 Genesis 11:6, NASB

35 Genesis 11:7, KJV

36 Numbers 14:27-30

37 Genesis 17:5; OT:85, Strong's Exhaustive Concordance of the Bible 1st ed. Copyright © 1988, by Hendrickson Publishers.

38 I Samuel 17:26, AMPC

39 Genesis 17:9-11

40 Matthew 9:21, NASB

41 OT:1288, Strong's Exhaustive Concordance of the Bible 1st ed. Copyright © 1988, by Hendrickson Publishers.

42 "advantage." *Merriam-Webster.com. Dictionary*, Merriam-Webster, https://www.merriam-webster.com/dictionary/advantage. Accessed 3 February 2020.

43 Genesis 1:28; Psalm 8:6

44 Genesis 9:1; Genesis 12:2-3; Genesis 22:16-18; Genesis 26:2-4

45 NT:2127, Strong's Exhaustive Concordance of the Bible 1st ed. Copyright © 1988, by Hendrickson Publishers.

46 These are examples: Genesis 9:1, Genesis 22:16-18 and Genesis 26:2-4.

47 OT:6213, Strong's Exhaustive Concordance of the Bible 1st ed. Copyright © 1988, by Hendrickson Publishers.

48 Deuteronomy 7:14

49 Matthew 18:10; Hebrews 1:14

50 II Corinthians 4:13, KJV

51 OT:8444, Strong's Exhaustive Concordance of the Bible 1st ed. Copyright © 1988, by Hendrickson Publishers.

52 Proverbs 18:8

53 Matthew 15:21-22

54 Acts 3:26; Romans 1:16

55 Matthew 15:27, KJV

56 Matthew 8:10

57 Judges 16:28, NASB

58 Judges 16:30

59 Mark 10:47, KJV

60 I Chronicles 17:14

61 Proverbs 15:1, NASB

62 Proverbs 23:7

63 Proverbs 13:3, KJV

64 Psalm 91:3-16

65 OT:7682, Strong's Exhaustive Concordance of the Bible 1st ed. Copyright © 1988, by Hendrickson Publishers.

66 I Samuel 17:45, KJV

67 Psalm 91:7, KJV

68 Numbers 22:4-11

69 OT:6895, New American Standard Exhaustive Concordance of the Bible with Hebrew-Aramaic and Greek Dictionaries. Copyright © 1981, 1998 by The Lockman Foundation.

70 "homoolgéo." NT:3670, Strong's Exhaustive Concordance of the Bible 1st ed. Copyright © 1988, by Hendrickson Publishers.

71 NT:3671, Strong's Exhaustive Concordance of the Bible 1st ed. Copyright © 1988, by Hendrickson Publishers.

72 "lego." https://biblehub.com/str/greek/3004; (14 March 2020)

73 Isaiah 46:10

74 Luke 1:20

75 Proverbs 21:23, KJV

76 Proverbs 13:3, KJV

77 NT:3525, Strong's Exhaustive Concordance of the Bible 1st ed. Copyright © 1988, by Hendrickson Publishers.

78 Job 1:7, KJV

79 OT:2600, New American Standard Exhaustive Concordance of the Bible with Hebrew-Aramaic and Greek Dictionaries. Copyright © 1981, 1998 by The Lockman Foundation.

80 Job 1:12; Job 2:6

81 Job 1:5, KJV

82 Job 1:21, AMPC

83 Job 1:21, KJV

84 "dread." *Merriam-Webster.com. Dictionary*, Merriam-Webster, https://www.merriam-webster.com/dictionary/dread. Accessed 9 November 2019.

85 Job 15:6

86 Job 8:2, KJV

87 Job 11:2

88 I John 1:9, KJV

89 Job 12:7-9

90 I John 1:5, KJV

91 Job 38:2, AMPC

92 Job 40:4, KJV

93 Job 42:6, AMP

94 OT:5162, New American Standard Exhaustive Concordance of the Bible with Hebrew-Aramaic and Greek Dictionaries. Copyright © 1981, 1998 by The Lockman Foundation.

95 Romans 2:4

96 Job 42:12

97 OT:3045, Strong's Exhaustive Concordance of the Bible 1st ed. Copyright © 1988, by Hendrickson Publishers.

98 Ezekiel 28:14

99 OT:7951, Strong's Exhaustive Concordance of the Bible 1st ed. Copyright © 1988, by Hendrickson Publishers.